Industrialution

Industrialution

◆

"the Experience Principles"

Dennis G. Lex

iUniverse, Inc.

New York Lincoln Shanghai

Industrialution
"the Experience Principles"

iUniverse, Inc.

For information address:
iUniverse, Inc.
2021 Pine Lake Road, Suite 100
Lincoln, NE 68512
www.iuniverse.com

ISBN: 0-595-31204-7 (pbk)
ISBN: 0-595-66273-0 (cloth)

Printed in the United States of America

To my wife, soul mate and best friend Barbara,
Who's constant support and love
Made this book possible.

Also to my daughter Mary and son D.G.
In recognition of their love and support

Contents

Foreword

The first industrial revolution started in the 19th century, evolved over time and peaked during the Second World War. America's industrial might was perceived as the mechanism that gave the allies the ability to win the Second World War. Following the war, "Japan Incorporated" came to America to understand the vast industrial capability that they woke up (or sleeping giant as their military described it). Wanting to regain its stature and become a world power, Japan benchmarked America, studied its manufacturing underpinnings, copied what they saw, improved on it, and started a Second Industrial Revolution. In the meantime, the western industrial giants had again fallen asleep and were lulled into complacency. By the mid 70's, Japan was well into a Second Industrial Revolution when they once again awoke the sleeping giant. This time however, the giant wasn't as nimble or as quick to respond. The response of the western world required a cultural change, and cultural changes take time. New mindsets had to develop and old paradigms had to be broken. Gradually, however, the inertia of the manufacturing culture was overcome and American and European Industry managers came, kicking and screaming, into this Second Industrial Revolution.

Today, however, with the advent of microprocessor technology, we are immersed in ongoing industrial revolutions with time frames from one to the next becoming shorter and shorter. These industrial revolutions are being driven at an unprecedented rate of change by an escalating accumulation and use of knowledge. We can no longer say whether we are in a third, fourth, fifth, etc. industrial revolution. We can only say we are in what I have come to believe is a constant **"Industrialution"**.

Consequently, "Industrialution" is forcing change in all areas of industrial operations. Plant operating techniques are harder to master. Microprocessors are driving knowledge at an accelerating rate and this accelerating knowledge is changing the way industrial managers must run manufacturing plants. Time has become the lost resource which industrialists had at their disposal during the first industrial revolution. It is this resource that allows one to gain experience.

New manufacturing techniques coupled with mega-mergers, consolidations, downsizing and global business requirements are driving managers of industrial operations around the world to adjust their operating techniques without the ability to gain experience from previous moves and decisions. They will not be able to learn by their mistakes and grow with the business. As a result, one of the major problems in industry today is the inability of plant operating teams to develop experienced human resources to operate manufacturing sites. It is this problem that this book attempts to address.

PREFACE

This book is a synopsis of my thirty-five years in manufacturing condensed in a way that will hopefully accelerate the learning curve of the reader. I highlight "experiences" which I contend will be constant over time and methods that will help the reader grapple with the constant accelerating rate of change in a plant. The book is directed towards those who must take leadership roles in manufacturing to assure the future of the business they operate for the employees, stockholders, and community.

Time is a necessary element to develop leaders in manufacturing. Plant teams must learn to handle constant transformation and reinvention. The "Industrialution Experience Principles" is a set of proven operating concepts that will hopefully transcend the time resource and give the reader a jump start on some of the leadership methods I believe are needed to operate a manufacturing plant. The thoughts presented are based on my experience and the significant observations I noted during my years in manufacturing. I contend these principles have been the stable underpinnings of running and managing plants in the past and will continue to be the principles necessary to manage future industrial operations.

Many of the concepts presented in this book are based on experience and could be the subject of stand alone books or doctoral dissertations. No extensive discussion of these principals can be aptly covered in this book. If I attempted that approach, you would loose the thought process for this book which is the power of the synergy of these principals when applied in total.

There are fifteen chapters in this book. Each chapter highlights a principle that is presented in a format which can be perceived as a learning lab. The final chapter is a summary of the fifteen experience principals and related key concepts. Hopefully the summary will serve as a future reference. Like the chapters in a text written to teach mathematics or the sciences, each chapter should be understood before proceeding to the next. For this reason, the first seven principles should be read in sequence. The remaining eight principles are subsets of the first seven and support, in more detail, the day to day actions necessary to run a plant. The final eight chapters do not necessarily require that they be read in sequence.

INTRODUCTION

Surviving "Industrialution" in manufacturing requires technique. The technique one must acquire is part management and part technical knowledge of the product and industry salted with just the right amount of gamesmanship. Like an athletic team, plant teams must learn the techniques for success and constantly train to become the best. When all the planning and strategizing is put aside, the objective of manufacturing is to physically produce products in a process that adds value.

Manufacturing is not held in high esteem today in most developed countries—with the two notable exceptions being Japan and Germany. A career in manufacturing in the United States and Great Britain is an under-rewarded, unappreciated existence. Therefore, to get someone to spend a career in manufacturing in order to develop the technique and skills to manage a plant becomes very difficult. Benchmarkers have long studied Japan to find answers as to how an entire country went from a war torn shambles to a mighty manufacturing machine. They continue to identify various operating elements but never identified or accepted the real driver. Japan Incorporated realized, after the Second World War, that one of the key underpinnings of the power in the United States during the war was its manufacturing abilities. They also must have realized, since it is ingrained in most of Japan's corporate culture, that the only way to survive in the world is to establish a mindset where a career in manufacturing is the only way to the top of the corporate ladder. This realization has been lost by many in the comfort of today's world.

I do not suggest that there is an option of changing the mindset or the culture of the business press, or attempting to stop the trends in industry downsizing, mergers, and globalization. Rather, this book addresses the effects of those external forces that are changing the ability of industry to ever again develop and nurture experienced manufacturing management teams. I will do this by attempting to short-circuit the development curve the baby boom generation possessed and leave the reader with some understanding of the key elements required to orchestrate life in a plant. My short circuit approach is addressed through the development of a set of "Experience Principles" or EP's. Hopefully, this will demonstrate that success in manufacturing requires the synergy of all the elements of manufacturing, which must be played out in the proper order at the right time in the life cycle of an industrial operation. Manufacturing in many respects is a true art form. Like a well orchestrated symphony that requires each instrument play at a prescribed time, each element in the life cycle of a manufacturing plant must be addressed at precisely the right time and with the proper emphasis if one is to achieve the mission of a manufacturer—**productive throughput**.

The challenges to running a successful industrial operation are enormous and without good press, it is becoming very difficult to capture and maintain the quality people that can drive continuous improvement. When I started working thirty-five years ago, I was a young inexperienced engineer entering into an environment where there were organizations full of veterans ready and willing to train me in the art of manufacturing. Today, the typical manufacturing plant is filled with inexperienced engineers and management teams. The veterans are becoming extinct. The ratio of experience to inexperienced manufacturing types has not only reversed, but the performance expectations are higher. Even the number of people employed by manufacturing plants has been dramatically reduced due to the trend in downsizing. The experienced manager no longer has the time (nor the motivation) to train novices knowing that if they have a sharp young intern, he/she most likely will move on to areas with a higher probability of advancement. The incoming young graduates are sharp and aggressive. But unlike the manufacturing types of recent generations, they read the Wall Street Journal, play with the stock market on their home computers, and are keenly aware of where their career ladders lead. They can read the signals and the expected outcome is obvious. They will not spend years perfecting their skills in manufacturing knowing that executive level jobs will not come from the manufacturing community. Young graduates will never learn the little nuances that are key to managing a successful manufacturing operation. There are new rules to the game writes Peter E. Carlson. "We are living in environments that are turbulent and unpredictable. Plants must survey under wicked dilemmas that are not clearly resolvable. There is no substitute for experience".

You will find vast collections of books and authors far more knowledgeable than I on each of the concepts address. But each author will write in depth on the specifics of their topic as if their element stands alone and the other keys to successful manufacturing do not exist implying irrelevance. Many of these books lead the reader to believe, even though it is not usually stated, that if they practice the theories and disciplines put forth, their business will be successful. Many imply that buzz words, like "Lean Manufacturing", will solve all problems. In reality, a manufacturing plant is a complex interaction of all of the buzz-word concepts and philosophies. The management team must never take their eyes off of any of the elements. Those most experienced in manufacturing will admit that life in the plant is like a circus. And like a circus, no one comes to see the plant operating team juggle just one of the manufacturing disciplines. Plant teams must think on their feet. That requires that all the concepts and the knowledge of manufacturing disciplines needed to run a successful operation be at their disposal.

Each chapter in this book is dedicated to what I believe to be a major experience principle. I have found that understanding concepts such as the experience principles presented in this book is one thing. However, applying them on the manufacturing floor is quite another undertaking. For this reason, I have elected to end up each discussion on a specific experience principle with a short narrative about a fictional manufacturing plant called EP Manufacturing. At the conclusion of the book, the reader could, if motivated, consolidate each story and have a short novel on the life and times in a typical plant.

Each concept in this book must be lived and practiced if one is to survive and grow a business. This book is written for plant management teams who must survive and operate within the changing business environment for manufacturing operations. These are the individuals who have no ability to control the outside forces that continually disrupt the structure and future of their facility, but have the authority and empowerment to drive all that happens within. The objective for a manufacturing team is clear—drive not for a plant of the future, but for one that is *a plant with a future*.

Experience Principle #1:
Define the Game

The mindset of the typical manufacturing person is a belief that corporate managers understand the underpinnings of all the little nuances that make a plant productive. In reality, corporate operating teams do not have the time, nor is it usually their function, to keep abreast of all phases of developments in technology and how these developments may apply to individual facilities in the company. That is why the manufacturing team in each plant in a corporation should take the responsibility to define the business strategy for the plant and make sure the company hierarchy is fully cognizant of that definition to insure integration into the corporate strategy. To do this, manufacturing teams must learn the corporate "game" and develop a plan for their specific plant. The game, simply stated, is how you get things done in your company. It will be different in each company.

To start development of a game plan, a plant needs to define a strategic position. Strategic positions can be based on customer needs, customer accessibility, or the various products or processes the plant has that can be presented as quality, technology or cost advantages. It is the human resource base working at the facility who know the details of the operation and technologies. They are the ones who need to define the strategic position and, on a defacto basis, the future role of the plant and its products. The objective of a plant team is to win, where winning is protecting the plant's future. And it is a given that the plants future only makes sense if it is for the good of the company and the people working at that location. However, you can't win if you don't play and you will play most successfully if you define the game and create a game plan.

To play the game of manufacturing you must know the rules for the system in which you operate. Or better yet, be proactive and define the rules of the game. Once you know the rules, you can develop the gamesmanship necessary to survive. People below the top level of any organization tend to believe they do not have or have very little ability to make decisions on day to day issues let alone long term strategic issues. In reality, they have far more ability than they think. And that is where playing the game comes into focus. Obviously, if you want to play the game and win, the best way to do it is define the rules to your advantage and then play more passionately than the other players.

Define Your Business...What Do You Do.

Define the game. What is it that a plant does? You may think this is intuitively obvious. But, beware of anything that appears intuitively obvious. Ask yourself and your peers simple questions that on the surface appear to be rather shallow——such as what is our business? What does the plant do? I am willing to bet there will be a lot of different answers. When one tries to put the obvious into words, it will be interesting to see the different definitions that develop. Let me explain. Each day a typical plant ships a product that it manufactures and/or assembles using some type of process. The first and most critical question to ask is: *should the business be defined based on the product it manufactures or by the process that manufactures the product?* For instance; assume this plant manufactures glass bottles. Is the plant in the bottle business, glass blowing business, glass business or the packaging/container business? When this question is answered, it leads to the next critical question: in what industry is the plant? The parent company of this plant may define itself as being in the container industry but the plant defines itself as being in the glass industry; or the company could be in the glass industry and the plant could be in the bottle blowing business. If the plant is in the glass business then the management team will not be interested in keeping up to date on the latest in plastic blow molding developments. But they will be very interested in developments in glass technology. If however, the plant is defined as being in the container business, then materials aren't the relevant common denominator and plant management must keep abreast of trends in containers, the materials for containers, and the equipment for manufacturing those containers. The broader you define your business, the broader the knowledge base required to stay abreast of all the related technologies.

The following story highlights the significance of these decisions. Many will remember that at one point in time, the average consumer believed the only real watches made were manufactured in Switzerland. A Swiss manufactured watch was about the only watch one could buy with perceived quality or reliability. Swiss manufactured watches would have easily been on top on any type of customer survey as a preferred product. However, over time, the Swiss watch industry lost significant market share following the invention of the quartz movement that gave way to the digital electronic watch. Japan Incorporated took major chunks of the watch industry market away from the Swiss. Most thought the Japanese invented the technology and got the jump on the Swiss. That wasn't the case. The quartz movement, which led to the digital watch, was developed and initially patented in Switzerland. That's right, the Swiss invented the digital watch.

Did Japan beat the Swiss to the market based on some manufacturing knowledge or in house process technology? I believe the answer is no. The mindset of the Swiss, based on what occurred, must have been a perception that a watch was a mechanical device with gears and analogue dials. They thought they were in the watch business. But in reality, whether it was on paper or not, the Swiss watch industry was in the business of manufacturing precision mechanical devices. The culture in the plants most likely could not identify with anyone that would buy or define a watch as anything but a mechanical device. Had the mindset and game plan defined the business as product related rather than process related, the day to day decisions would have focused on developments in watch technology and not the process of making watches. The game plan would have been different and the Swiss companies would most likely have aggressively taken the quartz movement invention to the manufacturing stage before the rest of the industrial world understood the significance of this development. Today, the Swiss watch industry might not have had to deal with competitors that did not exist (for all practicable purposes) prior to the invention of the quartz movement.

Another example comes from the steel industry. Those entrenched in the inner core of the steel industry perceived a steel plant as a fully integrated operation that took coal and iron ore from the boat and provided finished steel products. The facilities constituted a series of buildings that were, in effect, a small town. The investment in one of these plants was enormous. And as the operating costs to keep these albatrosses running became excessive, productivity offsets could not keep pace with customer pricing pressures. Inside the plants, the operating teams continued to bury their mindsets deeper into paradigms of what a steel plant was supposed to be instead of understanding new manufacturing technology and what could be done to guarantee continuing improvement in the plant performance. The metallurgists who kept an eye on new developments and belonged to the technical societies are the ones that should have had the responsibility to read the signals and pursue a new game plan. These in plant technical experts, like the Swiss, could either not get beyond their mindsets or did not believe that they had the responsibility to address technology and environmental changes which could be applied to new ways of making steel—but others did.

Perceptive individuals believed a steel mill did not require a source of iron ore, blast furnaces or BOF's (Basic Oxygen Furnaces) to make steel. They shed the paradigm of what constitutes a steel mill and concluded all that was needed was a good supply of steel scrap, an electric furnace, and a rolling mill. The result was the advent of the Mini-Mills that slowly started to take over the business base of the big steel mills. If the fully integrated steel mill operating teams had developed their own business strategy, did some benchmarking, and understood what could be done technically, many of the major mills could have opted to incorporate the mini-mill concept within the framework of the larger facilities. But that did not happen. As a result, thousands were laid off, steel towns died, and only after decades of pain are the large mills starting to come back—somewhat leaner than in the past. But not all the mills came back. Kaiser Steel had 15,000 employees in the late 50's, about the time of the last nationwide steel strike. Today, there are none. These examples highlight why it is so critical to define a plant level strategy.

Once you define the strategy, you can define the game plan. So you must decide if your business is based on:

- The plant's process?
- The materials used?
- The product it manufactures?

Regardless of which of the above is decided, the position taken will automatically lead to the detailed elements of the game plan. The details of the game plan will include decisions such as:

- Should money be spent upgrading existing facilities?
- Should old equipment be replaced with like technology as no new technological developments are on the horizon?
- Should plant processes be highly automated or manual?

What is the right decision? There is none. Each comes with a degree of risk. Taking a position requires trade-offs. Each decision creates the need for choice and purposefully limits what a company or plant can offer. By making these decisions, a plant is deterred from straddling on issues, developments and ongoing repositioning which degrades the value of the day to day activities of the plant's efforts. Consistency ensures that competitive advantages of activities do not erode or cancel themselves out. It also makes it easier to communicate what you are to your customers and your people. The operating people need a clear-cut understanding of the game plan as they are the ones who have to incorporate whatever plan is adopted.

Why Should Plants Play the Game?

The game plan is not only a definition of the business, but includes all the little nuances which some may define as the art of corporate politics. So why should those at the manufacturing level be concerned? If your plant is the only manufacturing facility in the company, then obviously whatever the plant does is "core" to the company. Thus it can be concluded that if the plant fails, the company fails. But if, as noted in the case of the glass bottle business example, the plant's perceived definition is not in line with the plant's parent company, the plant may not be core to the company's future. This means the plant could be closed or divested. Unfortunately, the answer as to whether a plant is core or non-core is never clear. Normally the answer is more of a perception that will only surface when the plant attempts to expand or requires some large investment. Then it is too late. A plant team needs to understand the plant's position in the company prior to moving ahead with major requests for investment or product and process changes. This requires that the plant develop a strategy, which means they must play the game of corporate politics.

As mergers and acquisitions evolve, specific plants with specific manufacturing technologies and processes could move from core to non-core and back depending on where the plant sits relative to other plants in the corporation. It takes a deep dive to find out if the plant is core and how the plant team can address its position. This deep dive necessitates finding out not only how the plant is perceived but also finding solutions to maintain the plant as a core facility. Or, it can mean finding out the company plans to divest itself of the plant no matter what its financial status is. An integral part of playing the game of manufacturing requires that a plant team aggressively keep abreast of how its' parent company is evolving and how the plant's facility and products can stay at the leading edge of the corporate mindset.

Being core equates to being perceived as critical to the long term viability of the company. It then usually follows that the manufacturing technology and processes will be supported from an investment standpoint. Money will be available if a plant is seen as key to maintaining competitive products. It usually means the financial hurdles for investment will be lower (the corporation will be open to lower returns) than if the operation is non-core. On the other hand, being non-core is to put it bluntly, ugly. A company will allow a plant's existence, at least more often than not, as long as it continues to generate a positive cash flow and can show that it is competitive with an outside alternative—but rarely for the long term. Being perceived or stated as a non-core operation in the company will require the plant to operate differently and have a different game plan.

A manufacturing operating team won't be able to understand the game it has to play to stay in business unless the team understands how the corporation makes decisions, establishes policies, manipulates the in-house system (the way things get done) and identifies the person that makes the decisions. In a corporation, decisions affecting a plant could be made several levels below the CEO or it could be at the CEO level. In a privately held company, the owners may be absentee owners with key decisions being made at some other operating level. In most cases it depends on the authority given to each organizational level in the company. There is a system no matter what the size of the company. If you know the system, you can manipulate it to the benefit of the plant or project the plant is trying to sell.

In one of the Dilbert sitcom shows (Dilbert is the cartoon character that mimics life in business), there was a scene where he takes two proposals to his boss. One is obviously the preferred proposal and the other is also as obviously unacceptable. When the boss asks him why he bothered making such an obviously unacceptable second proposal, Dilbert responded with the following: "upper management needs to think they are in charge of making decisions, so you need to give the boss an alternative to make him feel important". This cartoon, while simple, summarizes one game tactic. To get the proposal through the system, Dilbert had to play by the rules of the game he perceived for his company—rules he learned with experience.

<u>He Who Makes the Rules, Rules</u>

Devising the rules is the first rule of the game. To better explain gamesmanship necessary to play the game of manufacturing, a manufacturing team needs to ask questions about every aspect of the business including questions that on the surface seem obvious. Why? Usually the way in which a company system operates is not that obvious to all individuals. Most don't pay attention. This fact allows you to make the rules similar to the way Dilbert did. But you can't devise the rules unless you first understand the company and the system. To do that, you need to understand the answers to some key questions:

- **What is the plant's business?**

- **Which competitors should the plant benchmark?**

- **Who are the customers and what are their service needs?**

- **What is the plant's technology position?**

- **Does the corporation believe the plant has a future?**

- **Do the team members believe the plant has a future?**

- **Is the plant a cost center or a profit center?**

- **What level of financial approval authority does the plant have?**

- **Who has final approval authority? That person controls your destiny.**

- **How does the system work——does the plant sell in house to other company facilities, or direct to an outside customer? Is there opportunity to adapt to a new customer base?**

- **Which competitor is perceived as the best in the business and why?**

- **Is there a treasury function for your plant? If yes, then the plant can fund its own future. If no, the plant has to compete for investment money.**

- **Do manufacturing objectives take precedence over all other matters?**

- **Do managers in your facility periodically get developmental moves to other business units in the corporation? In other words, does the management team feel an alliance with the plant and its products?**

Once a plant manufacturing team understands how the system works, the team can start to outline the necessary gamesmanship. For instance; suppose a plant has always sold its products to its sister plant in the corporation (generally referred to as a tier 2 manufacturing operation) with low profitability. However, there are better opportunities on the outside. The plant does a little research and confirms that there isn't a corporate policy stopping the plant from selling to an outside customer (a tier 1 supplier) of the company. However, plants as a general rule do not have a sales function. So does the team ask someone not directly held accountable to the plant's performance and future if the plant can start selling its available capacity to an outside customer? Of course not—asking the question will require someone to define the rule as a rule may not exist. And since the person most likely asked does not have equity in the decision, in other words is not being held accountable for the plants profit and loss, the answer may not be in the best interest of the plant. So the plant must define the rule to its benefit. And in this case, the rule the plant defines is that it is an acceptable policy to sell to customers outside the corporation if there is profit to be made. Further, since the plant does not want to open up a major dialogue in the corporation by requesting marketing and sales support, it defines a second rule which is that it is okay to use a plant employee to handle the sales function and service support for that outside business. In this way, the plant now takes control of its own destiny. It made the rules—therefore it rules.

The Second Rule—Assume Nothing

Manufacturing people tend to assume that the corporation (or system) understands what each and every plant does in the company and how each of the respective plant's manufacturing expertise fits into the big picture—which is the corporate business strategy. Plant personnel assume the system (the system in a company is the bureaucracy and the people who can affect the future of the plant) understands the basics such as where the plants are located, something about each plant's employment statistics, products and technologies. But are these good assumptions? Your first thought, of course, is that they must know. However; let me share a story with you which gives light to this question—a story that really happened. I was working on a project with a raw material company when the company's senior management team decided to come to the plant to review our program. The plant was in Newark and the parent company's home office was located in the Northwest part of the United States. As is typical, on the day of review, the company's senior management for this division boarded the company plane and flew east to Newark. The plant management team in turn had cars at the Newark airport to pick up the management team. However, the plane never came or so they thought. Actually, the cars were waiting at the airport in Newark, Ohio, the plants location, and not in Newark, New Jersey where the plane landed. No one on the plant project team realized, or could have ever imagined, that the company's senior officers, let alone the flight crew of the company aircraft, did not have any idea in what state their plant was located. And, if they didn't know that, how could they be expected to understand the project, the needs of the plant, or the funds required for the program?

So who should have been held accountable for this problem? Should it have been the plant or the company management teams responsibility? I contend it was the plant's problem even though it is the tendency of plant personnel to hold staffs accountable. If you are part of the plant team, reality in a large corporation is that it is your mission to understand that there are no assumptions when it comes to expectations from who ever controls the purse strings or plans for your plant's future. Assume nothing is a key rule of the game plan.

The above example illustrates why you must define the game for your business. In the case of this material company, the first part of the game plan should have been to get some pre-reviews and visibility with senior management. Items such as what the plant made, human resource issues, plant location and the plant's business summary should have been reviewed in advance of the meeting. This executive summary should have been delivered to each of the appropriate managers making the trip prior to their departure.

A story about a Fictional Plant (EP Manufacturing).

At the close of each chapter, I have written a fictional story about a manufacturing plant which we will call EP Manufacturing—where EP stands for Experience Principle. The story will illustrate how the manufacturing team in EP addresses the concepts presented in each chapter. This approach will hopefully re-enforce the readers understanding of the concepts put forth in the chapter.

EP will be part of a Fortune 500 conglomerate that has many diverse businesses. In the current round of "Industrialution" this is becoming typical. For example: General Electric is in the appliance business, plastics business, manufactures diesel train engines and owns RCA plus a television network. U.S. Steel is not only in the steel business but also the petrol chemical industry. TDK, a Japanese company, known for video cassettes, has major manufacturing plants dedicated to plastic injection molding, makes magnets, and is a large manufacturer and supplier of electronic devices to companies that make electronic consumer products. DaimlerChrysler, a company most people view as being in the automobile business, also manufactures bicycles, trains, helicopters, airplanes and missiles. They are actually in the transportation and aerospace industry. The plant management team at DaimlerChrysler that makes bicycles must compete for investment capital out of the same bin and from the same board of directors that are making decisions on investing in the next generation of cars, trucks, and airplanes. You would have to believe that the bicycle plant is not going to get the funds for future investment out this group without an exciting game plan. Therefore, our fictional plant, EP Manufacturing, will be part of a major corporation in that same manor as the plants that are part of those companies noted above. Below are a list up assumptions to set up our fictional plant.

- EP, the plant, molds plastic toy products and assembles electronic circuit boards into molded products.

- EP sells their product as semi-completed toy modules to another division in the company that does the final assembly.

- EP is part of a large division in a corporation that has business in many industries (toys, electronics, duplicating machines, and raw composite materials).

- The manufacturing processes include injection molding, blow molding, and some minor circuit board soldering and automatic insertion of surface mounted capacitors and resistors. The plant does not incorporate wire bonding, or have thin/thick film technologies currently employed in most electronics business but believes it must if it is to survive.

- The customer is currently internal but could become external.

- The plant is located in a rural area 1000 miles from the world headquarters of the parent company.

- The plant has 500 employees, but given more space could expand as the opportunity for new products and technologies exists.

- The plant must get funding if it is to continue to grow and be a viable facility.

- Corporate management does not perceive EP as core to its future.

- EP is a profit center

- Corporate has a sales/marketing organization for toys which spends no time on EP's specific products.

- EP needs two new manufacturing technologies to establish long term competitiveness that require big investment and most likely a plant expansion. Corporate believes these processes and products can be purchased outside if necessary.

- The plant management team names and responsibilities are as follows:

  Dennis is the plant manager

  Mary is the controller

  DG is the engineering manager

  Barb is logistics and production control

  Vito is quality control

  George is the industrial engineer

  Harry is the production supervisor

  Bill is human resources

  Judy is accounting

EP's Story Part #1—The Game Plan

Dennis called the team together to discuss the future of the plant. He opened the meeting with some introductory comments: "electronics manufacturing technology is changing so fast that EP is going to need major chunks of investment in the future to stay viable. That means at some time in the near future our parent company will have the option to outsource the manufacturing services that are now core from EP".

"This observation", he said, "assumes that our board of directors doesn't want to spend money keeping up with technologies in electronics. Further I believe that when it becomes possible for new process technologies to be purchased outside the company, EP's value added advantage to the company for its products will drop dramatically and eventually the plant will no longer be needed. The plant's 500 people will be laid off and this small town we all live in will be hard hit. Many of us have friends and

relatives that will be affected. I see this as far off, maybe five years, but inevitable with the way technology is changing."

DG chimed in and asked "how do we establish a game plan to get major invest-ment for new technology and expand the plant knowing the politics and constraints of the system are not in our favor?"

Mary further highlighted the concern; "we will have to dig into the treasury bin which, rumor has it, marketing is currently tapping into for some pet projects."

Barb asked: "what is the probability, under any circumstances, to get funding for a business that is perceived non-core to the corporation?"

"Hold on a minute," Dennis said. "Obviously, we need a game plan. And by the way, we are not sure if the corporation sees us as core or non-core. However, we cannot assume anything. Whatever the mindset of the system, we must assume the worst and establish a plan that makes it clear that EP is a core plant for the future."

"Therefore, before we go further," DG observed, "we better define our business in a way that we can all agree on and feel comfortable will be the future for our plant."

"Keep talking," said Barb. "What are your thoughts?"

DG continued, "I think the team should define EP's business as the process by which the plant manufactures not the product we manufacture. We should define our business as the molding and assembly of electronic components to plastic molded sub-strates. EP can sell products to companies outside of the toy industry if necessary to sur-vive. By defining our business as the assembly of electronic components onto molded substrates, we can open the door to other market opportunities."

"I agree," said Dennis. "Any other thoughts on the subject?" No one had a better approach so Dennis asked for a vote. All agreed with DGs' recommendation.

With this decided, Barb suggested the first element of the game plan should be a mindset change aimed at the company's senior management people by working behind the scenes to convince marketing to advertise that toys made by EP's parent company are better because of EP's electronic processes. Barb said, "we want to convince the cor-porate marketing team that without EP's technology and processes, the parent compa-nies future will be questionable".

Dennis jumped in, saying "that is a good approach, Barb. Why don't you take on the assignment and figure out how we might approach the marketing department?"

"Of course behind this plant level marketing campaign," noted Mary, "should be an effort to develop technologies to make this become true or at least be perceived as true. Perceptions after all, are critical for staying in business. Stockholders may con-sider giving away the golden egg, but would hardly consider selling the golden goose that laid the golden egg. If the perception is that EP Manufacturing is a golden egg, it may be worth selling or trading for other investment opportunities." However, if EP

can create a mindset where the corporate system believes EP's manufacturing technology and know how is the golden goose, than that becomes a different story. Sell the golden goose and the corporation's future is eventually doomed."

"Good thought process", Dennis said. "That is an assignment for DG."

"Boy, I get all the easy ones don't I?" Said DG.

Accepting the fact that he was volunteered, DG started to think out loud, saying "the only immediate game plan tactic that comes to mind, and one we have at our disposal, is an approach I have seen work in other industries. It's big in Japan. I can best describe it as a patent everything strategy. The key is to submit patent, patents, and more patents. Even if most or all could be broken with little effort," said DG.

"Why is this a good tactic?" Barb asked.

"Because," said DG, "a lot of manufacturing companies that arm themselves with several patents, even if they are pending, force competitors to push the legal community to get involved. And lawyers will want to attack the patent issues one at a time and that will take them forever."

"You're right," said Dennis. "This will give EP the time we need to stay afloat until DG can develop new process technologies that will assure the plant's future."

"I get it," said Mary, "if we flood the system with patents we can put roadblocks in front of competitors and at the same time gain credibility from within the corporation."

DG added, "most credible competitors will go through legal channels and procedures to dispute patents even if they are pending. Not so ethical competitors may choose to ignore them and take their chances. But so what—our motivation is not to patent technology and keep ahead of the competition as much as it is to convince corporate management and the competition that EP is indispensable. All patents can and will be broken. However, patent submittals will give EP credibility and add to our one critical needed resource—time."

"Good game plan," said Dennis. "Lets go with DG's proposal and use the patent strategy as the second element of our game plan."

"Another reality that EP should consider," said Mary, "is that no matter how good EP's game plan, the corporation may still not accept the fact that EP's operation is core to the company's future. It may be that the best plan for the company would be to split off EP and sell the plant. They may recommend a spin-off or a merger. This could be the best approach if it becomes obvious that the parent company's mindset is to go in a different direction whether EP is profitable or not."

Dennis said, "unfortunately, we had better address Mary's concern. We can not assume even a good plan will mean the company will want to keep EP as part of the corporation. Therefore, Mary, you need to develop some proposals as part of our over-

all game plan. So we all agree, let me summarize what I think we have come up with as our game plan: EP will purse three strategies—first we must get marketing to back-door corporate and convince them EP is critical to the company's future. Second, there will be an effort to get a lot of patents into the system while DG starts to look at new processing technology. And third, we must consider the prospects of a spin-off."

"And by the way," said Mary, "success will be achieved when the marketing people start telling the corporation, indirectly, that their little plant is key to the corporations sales strategy."

Having completed the discussion, Dennis adjourned the meeting stating the team would re-convene to discuss the next level of detail–the business plan–at a later date.

Key Take Away Thoughts

As you slowly work your way through the mental gymnastics, you evolve into a game plan were the objective of the game is to win. Winning means staying in business. Staying in business means keeping up with "Industrialution" and being passionate about it. The game players all work in your company and have equity in the outcome. As you experience each principle in this book you will build on the game plan. You must examine these annually if you are to manage your manufacturing facility wisely. This, of course, becomes difficult to prioritize. You must do this during your day job—which is to get your product out the door. So remember the following:

- Identify your plant's expertise. Is it based on product, process or material?

- Understand you have to play the game of corporate politics to survive.

- He who makes the rules, rules.

- Assume nothing.

- Play the game passionately.

I will expand more on the need for game plans in each area as we go through the book and discuss the specifics for other experience principles. Hopefully, you will understand why you must, as a manufacturing type, never take your eye off the business part of running a manufacturing plant.

Experience Principle #2: Bureaucracy Brinkmanship is Critical

The "Random House Dictionary" explains a bureaucrat "is an official who works by fixed judgement without exercising intelligent judgement". The normal mindset by a plant and its management team is that these are the individuals who are either the owners of your business, the upper management team or for lack of a better understanding, the corporate system. Plants also tend to assume that the bureaucracy makes decisions on a facility based on fixed judgement that may not include the details of business or the real opportunities. The assumption is the bureaucracy is not privy to the plant's game plan leaving their destiny in peril. This will be true if you let it. And if you let it, it will control you. Therefore, your mission as a plant person is to control the bureaucracy.

My experience has led me to believe that the plant operating team not only has the ability but also the authority to dictate the destiny of their business. Referring back to the definition of a bureaucrat, plant people must accept the fact that they are a big part of the bureaucracy, and in fact could be all of it. If you have a salary job in a plant, I can assure you that the hourly work force perceives you as "top management" and associates you with the bureaucracy. They, the plant floor people, see plant level management teams as the cause of all they see wrong with the operation and its future.

I find that typical companies rarely have long term strategies for their plants, but are great at pursuing short-term operational improvements. That is why you must take control of the perceptions and business opportunities or plans that form this fixed judgement. Without it, the decision matrix will include input from parties less interested in your plants future, such as your competitors and the stakeholders in your operation (the owners or stockholders), who, by definition, will always question if funding your plant's future is the best use of the company's funds. Of more concern, the trend within corporations today is to build market capitalization rather than building companies and plants. That 's were brinkmanship becomes critical. You have to find a way to stay ahead of the bureaucracy or it will control your future.

Without distinctive strategic plant level plans, plant operating teams and their staff functions can become trapped in mutually destructive battles and develop a culture where strategy is not in the box of tricks for competing long term. In a competitive global arena, this drives a manufacturing operation toward costly mediocrity and mediocrity in the world of "Industrialution" means you will go out of business. Your mission is to pursue opportunities—get ahead of the bureaucracy or you will become the bureaucracy. If you don't stay ahead, life will be brutal.

Develop a Business Plan

Those who are given a mission to manufacture do not normally consider the business element. They normally conclude that the sole goal in the plant level organization is to get whatever product they manufacture or assemble out the door. In the short term, this thought process simplifies the responsibility and mindset of those who live and work within walls of a manufacturing operation. In the long term, it is the surest way to the inevitable end to the life of your manufacturing operation. This mindset will not meet the objective every manufacturing management team should have both for their stock holders, owners and employees:

-To guarantee your plant has a future and,
-Continuous improvement (short term productivity enhancements)

Manufacturing teams must beware of today's trend in what is referred to as corporate disintegration: the effort by corporate hierarchy to sell off or close all which they, at their knowledge level, believe is not core to the future of the company. You must take control of the mindset of the bureaucracy that is driving the future of the manufacturing operation——where you spend more time than you do with your family. And you must make sure the business plan for your plant is supported by and internally consistent with the rules you developed for your game plan. This plant level business plan does not have to be complex or detailed. It is a document that will be used to inform all who work in the plant and those outside the plant that need to know (such as staff, suppliers, etc.) as to the plant's future. In general, it should be more strategic than financial.

Long lead times are required to acquire and launch new products, assets, technologies and address paradigm shifts in all aspects of the operation. Only those at the plant level have a good feel for the time, resources required and issues associated with change. That is why it is your mission to recognize trends in processing, equipment, labor relations concepts, etc. and have your plans and projects defined before it becomes intuitively obvious to your competitors, the national press or the industry analysts. *When your industry is aware of a technological trend, you are behind and your operation is at risk.* A company will only outperform its rivals if it can establish a difference that it can preserve. Operational effectiveness (performing similar tasks and processes better than your rivals thereby getting more out of your imputes) is the key to the ever shifting productivity frontier and why you must always keep your eye on the trends in your industry and stay ahead of the competition. What you don't want to happen is to read about your plant's future in the local newspaper such as the article entitled *"Dana to Dump Factory"* which appeared in the August 12, 1999 Detroit Free Press;

> Toledo, Ohio supplier, Dana Corp. said it plans to sell its Marion, Ohio forging factory which was acquired as part of its 1998 purchase of Eaton Corp's heavy axle and brake business. The plant employs about 300 people and had $50 million in sales in 1998, Dana said, adding that the forging operation not longer fits its strategies.

With the pace of technology accelerating, the evolution of industrial plants, the layout of the physical plants and processes will change dramatically every few years. If the plant doesn't change, this is a clear signal that the business element is not keeping up with the evolving pace of technologies in products and processes. Corporate level finance groups, business strategists, marketing/sales and a company's board of directors understand this but do not have the expertise, nor the desire, to do the deep dives necessary. Deep dives into all aspects of a product and its processing is needed to understand the dynamics of technological changes and how those dynamics relate to manufacturing processes. This knowledge will be necessary to drive the future viability of the operation. There are megatrends in every element of a business. Yours is to understand the megatrends in manufacturing and address them early on.

The 2 Year Time Frame

Keeping ahead of the bureaucracy means thinking ahead, planning ahead, and working ahead. Something plant people do not want to do or think they have to do. My experience led me to conclude that if you think and plan two years ahead, that is about as good as you can effectively do in a manufacturing operation. Most likely you are barely ahead of your competitors since you have to assume they are also trying to keep ahead of you and have their own technology and/or cost cutting opportunities programmed. If you believe you are three or four year years ahead and can verify a leadership position in new product concepts and technology, you most likely have put yourself into a very costly position to sustain. If you want to be the leader in a manufacturing technology or product technology, your investment will always be higher than your competitors. I believe that if you read the trends, you can take a fast follower position and still stay ahead. A fast follower is one who does not have the costly R&D expenditures required to invent technologies, but one who is quick and nimble to respond. Japan Incorporated taught us how to play this game. Perceptions are important—yours is to make sure your customer and you parent company believe you are competitive and a step ahead of the alternative, whatever that may be. I will expand on this concept in a later chapter.

Protecting the Business

Your business plan may not necessarily be in line with the parent company or the owner. Plants, however, need time to re-engineer themselves and this requires they play some business games while the business plan is developing and being implemented. You need to stay open during alterations—which means you have to stay ahead of the bureaucracy. This necessitates that a plant continue to show productivity improvements while it simultaneously protects the plant assets that are projected to be needed for future technologies, products or processes.

Sometimes, however, plants keep a major facility in operation too long and it becomes a negative asset to the manufacturing operation dragging down a plant's ability to bring in new technology or re-align processes to a more lean and productive type of manufacturing operation. Technology moves on and plant assets get outdated. Accepting this becomes difficult since the only alternative is to scrap or sell off the asset and write it off the books. If it is a costly event, it will become a politically hard pill to swallow. Usually a more attractive approach is to abandon the facility in place. I have seen this approach many times and found it just makes the business worse the longer one avoids the inevitable. And since you continue to depreciate an asset you don't use, it makes the business look worse than it is.

EP's Story Part #2—Controlling the Bureaucracy

Dennis called his team together for the next round of discussions related to the plant's future. This time, to talk about the next phase in the evolving saga of EP Man-ufacturing—taking control of the bureaucracy. Dennis opened the meeting and said, "DG got his engineering team together and told them he wanted at least one patent write-up from each individual. From that list, he and I got together and identified at least four potential areas for patents."

"What surprised me," said DG, "is that these were all areas in which we could get patents. So it appears we have been lax at not teaching our people about the probabil-ity and importance of patents."

"I also have something going on relative to our little in house marketing game plan," said Barb—not to be left out of any attaboys that may be going around. "But give me a few more days while I bounce it off of some outside consultants Mary and I talked to about for help on marketing approaches."

"Good," said Dennis. "But we better get on with the next effort which means we need a need a good business plan and a strategy to hold off the wolfs while we imple-ment the business plan actions."

"How about a little open dialogue and get everyone's thoughts out before we lay out a rough draft of a business plan," said Dennis. Before he opened up the floor for dis-cussion, however, Dennis stated that the EP's business plan would be simple and to the point—no longer than one or two pages. He said that the financial projections have to be done annually anyway for corporate so it should not be a major incremental work-load for Mary's department. The document should be strategic as it would mainly be used as an in-house communication tool.

DG opened the dialogue with the following comments: "our strategy for the long term should be to keep fully integrated. I think we should maintain all the processes we have and keep them in place. However, injection molding has had a lot of produc-tivity improvements. As a result, we have been able to open up capacity. We should fill the open capacity until we can develop the new technology and-"

Mary stopped DG, saying "with the typical financial system burden allocation the company makes me use, the parts being made now carry more fixed costs than if the machines were fully utilized since the operating machines are carrying the burden and fixed costs of the machines that are sitting idle. As a result, if we bid on new work, I will have to include a higher fixed cost base. This will affect our ability to competitively price. Winning new business will be difficult."

"I understand," said Dennis. "However, let's hold that thought and continue the dialogue before we address this issue."

Barb said, "I came across some articles in one of the industry magazines we get discussing trends in molding and electronics. Yes, I passed them on to DG, before you ask. In a nutshell, what the articles highlighted was that, based on all the trends in molding and electronic related industries, the day is coming when the most productive way to make some of these new electronic toys will be to mold the electronic circuits onto the plastic inside the molding machines."

DG commented' "Yeah, I read the article and it looks like this will be accomplished through a yet to be developed process (at least undeveloped for the product we are manufacturing based on the knowledge we have in EP) of insert molding flexible electronic circuit boards in a molding machine."

"Therefore I could conclude," said Dennis, "that we have to hold onto all the injection molding machines or we may not have a future."

"Which means," said Mary, "we have to find a way to protect our molding capacity until we can show better utilization when the new process technologies are operational in the plant."

"Good discussion," said Dennis. "So let me summarize what I think I heard and tell me if you all agree. EP has open capacity that affects our ability to bid for new business. Good business sense would dictate that we sell the excess equipment to get it off our books. That would approve our bottom line today. A second issue you have discussed is that the new manufacturing technology that is coming may put us out of business completely if we don't jump in and develop it for our plant."

"And to make it more complicated," said Mary, "if we sell off the machines that are not being used, we won't have open capacity to launch and try out this new technology. So we can't get business because of the excess capacity, but we can't risk getting rid of the capacity since we won't have equipment for the new processes."

"To make it even more complex" said Dennis, "I have to assume that the corporation may not see us as core and won't let us buy new machines if this technology comes to pass."

Barb jumped into the conversation. "What a mess; it's going to take a very unique strategy."

"You're right, Barb. But what do we do?" asked Dennis. "Any ideas?"

"What I think we should do," said Mary, "is protect those machines by keeping the costs out of sight."

DG, looking surprised, said, "how do you do that? Won't it show up in the details of the financial schedules?"

"Of course it will," said Mary. "However, we can make the financial returns look much better for molding by skewing a bigger share of the plants overhead costs towards the electronic processes."

Barb asked, "doesn't that make the electronic side of the business look worse that it might be?"

"Yes it does," Mary answered. "But in today's culture, everyone is in love with electronics and I will assure you that processes and products associated with the manufacture of electronic components can take a lot more heat from the bureaucracy. This means management will live with poorer financials for electronics than molding since they believe electronics is the wave of the future. All we will do is take advantage of those perceptions to give DG time to bring home new technologies to support our little marketing effort and game plan we discussed in the last meeting."

"Okay," said Dennis. "I am all ears. How do we do this little maneuver and what are these costs you're going to skew."

"Plant controllers have a lot of flexibility in the burden rate allocation arena," Mary noted. "In fact, we have to bin the costs somewhere and the only rule is to bin them where it makes sense based on what products should absorb the costs. By bin I mean that the cost for items such as fork lift truck drivers could be allocated to the end item, or the plastic manufacturing or to electronic manufacturing. There are a lot of nebulous costs that can almost be justified in any bin and that is what I plan to do. What I will do is allocate cost items a little differently than we had done in the past. Here is a list I wrote down as we were talking."

- *Bin a bigger portion of the EP's warehouse space to electronics*

- *Expand the allocation of the total number of employees in the plant's indirect labor category to an electronic burden center*

- *Move the bulk of the building heating and other utility costs to electronics*

- *Bin the shipping and receiving areas to the total assembled final product*

- *Set up our plant departments such that the bulk of salary allocations go to electronics*

- *Corporate cost allocation, which is usually the costs for the parent companies headquarters, offices, marketing and sales, etc can also be skewed towards the electronics side of the business*

"*Can this be done in line with most finance procedures?*" asked DG.

Of course," Mary replied. "*In fact it has to be done. Somebody has to make a decision on how cost get allocated and you will usually find it is the lowest level person in your plants finance department that takes the responsibility and usually that person does it with less knowledge of the operation than the management team. Managers tend to believe there is a magical binning process developed that these people follow. This is not the case. The only people who really understand the details of the business sufficiently to be able to bin costs and do a decent job work in your plant. It is usually considered a little detail by plant management but should be just opposite—it should be addressed as a major detail and one that management spends time on and votes on how the allocations get binned. It has a major effect on long term decisions and the perception of the plant's various products and processes as you can see from our dialogue on this issue.*"

"*Good strategic thinking Mary,*" Dennis said. "*Do what you can in line with acceptable financial procedures for all our cost projections and budgets and, hopefully, we will keep the corporate mindset on other issues for the time being.*"

"*Next item,*" said Dennis. "*Since we are going to continue to assume that EP's corporate heads do not see molding as core to the company's future, it is unlikely they will give the plant funds or an organization to work on the advance developments necessary to be successful. This means we need a skunk works.*"

"*What's that?*" asked Barb.

Dennis responded. "*A skunk works is usually an out of the way confidential development operation that is not part of the mainstream staff operations or plant operations. Sometimes management knows about them and will unofficially support them and sometimes they don't. In EP's case, I suggest we fund an out of sight, out of the way operation in a separate building. Using my authority to spend up to $100,000, we should have enough money to support this project.*"

"*I have an idea,*" said DG. "*We can take one of our old machines out of service and start development on this new technology. I think I can furnish one or two of my engineering personnel and the plant can free up one or two of the key hourly skilled trades. This will be sufficient to start this little skunk works development program.*"

"*We can give this team a very clear objective,*" Dennis said. "*Bring in this new technology and make it production worthy. And they have to achieve this before EP's customer moves on to next generation products. When this is accomplished, EP can promote this technological breakthrough as a new electronic process which will give the plant a more viable future and long term competitive advantage.*"

"*Sounds good to me,*" said Mary. "*And I think we have enough money in our spending budget to support this program. Let's do it.*"

"The last thing we need to address," said Dennis, "is the concept of design for manufacture. It is something our company does not do well. Japan incorporated has made it an art form while it still gets talked about in other areas of the world. EP's situation is no different. Our plant will be more productive if we can get the toy developers to design the next generation products around EP's manufacturing processes and capabilities. No two plants process the same product the same way nor do they have individuals with identical expertise and capabilities. We need to get the designers to develop products and designs around EP's process and technology expertise. At the same time, DG's skunk works team should work closely with the designers to incorporate their future products around the new process technologies our team is trying to develop."

Barb said, "I get it. This design for our manufacturing processes will give us the ability to develop a long term competitive advantage versus whatever outside supplier might be considered to take over our business. Therefore, as EP develops this new technology for insert molding of electronic components, we need to simultaneously sell the concept to the product designers and marketers."

"You're right on," said Dennis. "Any more ides on the business plan strategy? Okay then, let me summarize our plan for the business and protect our current sourcing while we implement our strategy. And as I summarize, I think you will all see that what we are doing is taking control of the bureaucracy. Mary, it is your assignment to put this on one sheet of paper so we can talk about it to all our employees.

First—we concluded that it was necessary to <u>think ahead</u>. This Mary will do by moving burden rates to protect what was expected to be valuable assets for the future.

Second—Our team is <u>planning ahead</u> by funding the skunk works to give EP a viable technology for the future.

Third—DG's team will be <u>working ahead</u> with the product designers to get the new designs based on our manufacturing technologies."

Barb said, "now I understand how we are taking control of the bureaucracy or system if you want to call it that. We will have all of this effort going on behind the scenes and at the same time be in line with corporate procedures and policies. When the corporation's marketing team reach the realization that the next trend in toy manufacture is integrating the electronic circuits into the plastic housings, EP will be there with the process."

<u>Key Take Away Thoughts</u>

Staying ahead of the bureaucracy takes leadership. You must increase your flexibility. Eliminate words like should and shouldn't, right and wrong, and do not use phases like I agree or do not agree. You want to change your focus to meet objectives and solve problems by closing your eyes to the day to day clutter that takes your mind off the long-term objectives.

- Remember you are part of the bureaucracy.

- Plants are empowered more than they think when it comes to doing business planning.

- Develop a business plan for your plant. Re-do it every year.

- Play the games necessary to keep your plant in the best light.

- Think/plan for two years ahead.

- Understand your cost structure.

You also need to remember that while you are working on the future of the plant, you need to accomplish short-term objectives. A manufacturing team needs small wins in order to keep motivated to continue. Get resistance to change out in the open so you can deal with it and address the root cause of people wanting to stop you from making changes that will keep the plant ahead of the bureaucracy. Many times your underlings will link with the old ways of doing business since it is safer and they hope it won't affect career paths.

Experience Principle #3:
Benchmark or Self-Destruct

Once you understand your business, you must start to understand your competitors and others with similar processes and products. To do this you have to periodically benchmark. Benchmarking is a procedure whereby you identify and study the details of your competitors systems to identify productivity opportunities, new ways of processing, technology and gaps that may exist between your operation and the competition. It also can be used to establish your competitive edge if you have one and give you a feel for whether you are ahead of the competition. Companies that do financial benchmarking of other companies usually have the ability to take a more straightforward approach as much of the information is public. Key data sources are available from annual reports and other public sources such as the Bloomberg Report and Dun & Bradstreet.

On the plant level, however, benchmarking requires a more ingenious and detailed look at the underpinnings of a manufacturing's operational metrics—the little nuisances that the competitors believe are paradigms of their business and the culture that drives their system. Based on my experience, the meaty information you need to know is never available in technical papers, revealed at symposiums or discussed in the public sector—unless it is last years technology. So you must benchmark. And, benchmarking a manufacturing operation will only be beneficial if you grind out the details. There is no easy way.

Who Should You Benchmark

You need to not only benchmark your competitors, but plants in other industries as well. For instance: assume you are in the business of assembling plastic/steel components with some electronic controls and motors. The physical size of your final product can be important as it dictates the size of the facilities and the plant that produces those produces. Who would you benchmark to get some processing tips, learn some new manufacturing technology and make plastic housed products that incorporate some electronic functions? Two companies that assemble a product that meet the criteria are General Electric and Xerox. General Electric assembles appliances and Xerox assembles copy machines. A dishwasher has a plastic tub, a motor, electronic circuitry, and touch pad controls, etc. A copy machine has plastic panels, motors, electronic circuitry, touch pad controls, etc. Each company is in a different market. Each developed their own processes for their plants. Benchmarking each of these company's manufacturing facilities can give you a lot of insight on the way products are processed in different industries. Since you are in manufacturing, the product identity is not as important as the process. Also, since companies such as those mentioned above don't compete, it is more likely that key data would be discussed.

Another key item to understand is that a product and its process do not necessarily require the same technological awareness. An electronics assembly operation requires a understanding of mechanical, metallurgical and industrial engineering disciplines. The process engineer *does not need* to understand how to design and develop an integrated circuit to successfully process an electronics manufacturing plant. These are some of the key reasons why you must first understand who you are and spend time deciding how you should define your business. As we discussed earlier is this book, your definition may be different from the perception of the product development people and/or the shareholders.

Getting Ready To Benchmark

The first step and the most critical step in benchmarking is getting ready to benchmark. Once you are ready to benchmark, the actual benchmarking process becomes secondary. Why? Because once you have gone through an intensive benchmarking program, you will begin to believe that as much as you think you understand your own processes and operating system, your familiarity with the plant tends to blind you to those little nuances that are so important for improving competitiveness. These opportunities you will tend to find and see more clearly when you are looking at someone else's process that manufactures and/or assembles the same part. Working day to day in a plant will slowly deteriorate your observation skills such that what should be obvious process flaws and opportunities can not be seen. As the saying goes, you can no longer see the trees through the woods. That is why periodic benchmarking is such a great benefit.

I had one experience that highlights these recommendations. I was working in a plant that housed a highly automated chrome plating automotive bumper operation which had a major warranty problem. A small but significant number of parts were coming back where the plating was not adhering to the steel substrate. Of course our team constantly checked our the equipment and everything appeared to working according to the process. In hindsight, discovered that our competitors never had the problem—as at that time we had never heard of or understood the concepts and benefits of benchmarking. Had benchmarking been one of the tools on our radar screen, our first step would have been to revisit the detailed operation of our internal process to prepare ourselves for the questions we needed to ask and the observations we wanted to make during a benchmarking trip. My feeling is we would have found the problem. However, we didn't.

What we did finally conclude after two years, was the need to get a fresh eyes look——which in effect is a form of reverse benchmarking. Someone else, with experience, benchmarks your process and then tells you the results. To do this, I got a hold of one of the company's research chemists who was familiar with chrome plating technology. He benchmarked the process and than asked us where we were looking for the root cause of the problem. After I identified the steps the team had taken, he said something very interesting: "I will conclude that you have done your homework and verified that everything in your process checks out according to the proper way of running a plating process. Therefore, I will assume you are looking in the wrong place for the problem and I will look somewhere else". He did just that and found the problem two days later. A problem we could not find for two years. The problem was not in our plating solutions, which we had assumed, but rather in a water rise operation. He found the acid/base ratio was off but it only happened in the process when the automated chrome platter broke down and the parts sat for a period of time in the water rinse tank. The solution to the problem took an hour to fix. It only required the addition of an overflow pipe to keep the water chemically in balance. A multi million dollar warranty problem was fixed. Had we walked through another chrome plating operation (which we did at a later date), we would have seen that they all had overflow pipes.

Life in a manufacturing operation in today's environment is one that is full of continuous major operating issues requiring immediate action—and usually this means there is little time left in the day to think. The longer you have worked in your facility and the more experience you accumulate doesn't necessary mean you understand your process or plant better. It usually means just the opposite since human nature drives employees to developed a mindset over time which helps to built up paradigms that stymie change. That is the major driver for benchmarking in the manufacturing arena and why it is so important. It will force you to revisit your process and ask all the questions of yourself that you expect to get from your competitor when you visit their facility. In fact you will find that the actual benchmarking visits become secondary as you have found out so much about you own process that the preparation makes the exercise worthwhile.

What You Don't Find Is Just as Important

Your ability to benchmark is not that easy. You must dig for all the detailed questions and sometimes you can not get the answers no matter how hard you try. But this may be just as important an answer. You just may be better that the other company. For example; I visited Japan to benchmark the electronics industry and noticed all the plants were small factories. Plant sizes and expansion was constrained by land values and population densities, or so I concluded. Floor space was in hundreds or thousands of square feet, not millions, unless the product had to do with the steel industry, chemical industry or was an automobile assembly plant. The conclusion my team assumed was that the cost of land and the culture in Japan to work in small groups drove company managements to build small plants—or so it would seem as the reason. However, in northern Japan, I found a radio manufacturing operation that was comprised of several small plants on a large parcel of land. Standalone buildings were built within 20 yards of each other. Land area was not an issue as the plant had acres and acres of undeveloped land within their campus area. The plant was in the country on a fairly flat piece of land and the company fence line indicated they had a lot of spare property. Any American or European manufacturer would have put all the plant operations under one roof. It did not appear that the company had any of the constraints of companies that had plants in the high population areas of Japan. My benchmarking team, obviously puzzled, asked at our exit meeting why they limited their manufacturing floor space and the overall size of their physical plant? Why did they build several small plants (departments in our plants), when they could have built one big plant? Were the building sizes based on process steps, types of technology, or number of people? Our plans at that time were to build a new radio manufacturing plant in Canada and we were looking for new concepts in manufacturing from plant size to the level of technology.

However, the management team of the Japanese radio plant never answered the question to our satisfaction. After asking the same question using a different approach, we finally concluded that they did not answer because the Japanese managers truly didn't understand the question. Today I have come to believe, after several more benchmarking trips and more experience, that this radio plant management team had their paradigms just as we do. There may have been a reason at one time, but it had long passed. Plant management teams in most any culture suffer from much of the same problems we all have—they build and process plants in a certain way because this is the way it has always been done.

How To Benchmark a Manufacturing Plant

Getting ready to benchmark is the key. Getting ready means you must define your tools, the benchmarking process, and the measurements you will employ. First you must put together a benchmarking team. The optimum team would include all the disciplines. A manufacturing engineer, a design engineer, an analyst, and a fourth individual depending on what makes sense from your business. Beyond four team members, you will start to get resistance from most plants you want visit. Once your team is established, you must lay out your expectations. Prepare an agenda and get concurrence from the company you plan to visit. Have them review and comment. With their concurrence, the team can now go to work. The team must prioritize its outputs, and make judgment on how detailed the data needs to be so that the information will be in a useful form.

- What metrics do you want to measure?

- How do you plan to measure success?

- What will be the necessary quality level of the data you receive to make your benchmarking exercise successful?

One of the team members should be assigned to get as much information as possible on the facility and company you plan to visit. This should be done before you go into a competitors plant so that all you need to do is observe the manufacturing details that can not be obtained ahead of time from outside sources.

Benchmarking will require metrics a plant team is not used to keeping thinking about or monitoring in their own operation. This will be determined when you benchmark your own process prior to the trip. Listed in Table 1 is a checklist of all the things one must consider during a benchmarking trip. As you can see, the list is long and it will be unlikely you will be able to fill in the blanks for all the information noted. However, you will be surprised how much you can conclude.

• Name of Company	• Contacts	• Location Year
• Revenues	• Organizational Structure	Established
• Profits	• Labor Classifications	• Site Location
• Burden	• Salary/Hourly	• Distance to Customer
• Cost Structure	Breakdown	• Mode of Transport
• Support Facilities	• Number of	• Building Construction
• Materials Used	Operators/Facility	• Environmental Issues
• Assembly or	• Relationship to Parent	• Ceiling Heights
Manufacture	Company/Division	• Shipping/Receiving
• Products ... Why	• Average Age of	System
• Supply Base	Salary/Hourly	• Plant Size Policy
• Degree of Vertical	• Wage Rates	• Level of Equipment
Integration	• Fringe Benefits	• Degree of Automation
• Breakdown of Product	• Shift Pattern	• Policy on Automation
by Materials, Labor, and	• Level of Cross Training	• Number of Machines
Purchased Parts	• Number of	• Size of Machines
• Process Bottlenecks	Classifications	• Material Handling
• Batch Size	• Quality Systems	Systems/Degree of
• Cycle Times	• Customer Interfaces	Automation
• Machine Uptime and	• Test Facilities	
Definition of Uptime		
• First Time Through		
Good Parts		

Table 1. Benchmarking Checklist

Why would any plant or company give out the information listed above? The answer, obviously, is they wouldn't. But it will be very surprising how much of this information you can collect. You will get to a fairly good cost assessment if you use the data you get from the benchmarking trip and merge it with the data that is available from other industry sources such as raw material suppliers and/or equipment suppliers.

• You can get the cycle time of the equipment as you walk through the plant;

• Identify the labor rates which, surprisingly, most companies will tell you;

- Count the number of people adding value to the product (direct labor);

- Estimate how many people are supporting the manufacturing line such as fork lift truck drivers, quality inspectors, maintenance, etc (indirect labor);

- Get the age of the building and type of equipment.

From the above information, you can put together a fairly accurate product cost projection. You can use your own material and purchased part costs. Then if you know the type of manufacturing equipment, its brand and when it was purchased plus the age of the building, you can back into depreciation and maintenance costs. The items that you may not get, such as corporate assessments and marketing costs, are not as important to a plant operation. Your objective is to benchmark a manufacturing process and not necessarily a company.

Tricks to Benchmarking a Plant

Trick One can best be described by the market condition changes in the early 70's, when the American and European auto industry's market share was heavily attacked by Japan Incorporated. Numerous benchmarking trips were made to Japan by all domestic car manufacturers. This in turn was supplemented with many industry observers. Observations from those benchmarking trips in the early years led the auto industry as a whole to believe that Japan's industrial manufacturing procedures and concepts were the major threat. New manufacturing practices were identified such as Quality Circles and Just-In-Time inventory control concepts. One unfortunate conclusion was a perception that all of Japan's manufacturing infrastructure was alike and, therefore, all Japanese companies were efficient and forward thinking.

When looking back, however, most everyone who went to Toyota City in the 70's and all the early benchmarking trip conclusions were drawn from companies who had visited the same location. And at that time, Toyota City just happened to have one of the most forward thinking manufacturing management teams in the world. But without other company visits, the conclusions focused on the Japanese culture as key to Japan's manufacturing prowess more than the fact that Toyota was good. As a result, many productivity opportunities were not implemented by the early benchmarkers. They concluded that the culture of the Japanese people was the competitive advantage and therefore assumed nothing could be done in their own facilities to offset that advantage. This was obviously a wrong conclusion.

As time evolved, more and more trips were made and it became evident that like any other country, some of the Japanese auto companies were very good at what they did and some were no better and in fact worse. The good news was that these early benchmarking teams visited one of the best. Only after the Japanese auto industry came to America and started applying these same manufacturing philosophies, only this time using American workers, did benchmarkers begin to realize that culture wasn't the root cause of Japan's productivity advantage. So 'Trick One' in your benchmarking strategy is to visit several facilities—some you think are better and some which may not be. Understanding the difference between good and poorly run companies and attempting to understand mismanaged plants may be as meaningful as attempting to understand a successful company.

'Trick Two' is a key data sources and the most important part of a benchmarking trip when your inside a manufacturing facility—and that is **read the walls**. There is more good data on the walls of plants and machines in the form of charts, communication to plant personnel, blue prints of upcoming products and new equipment and general company information than you will find in an annual report or a marketing brochure. Plants and the people in those plants, worldwide, have a common phobia—they hang key company information and plant data on some vertical surface for all the employees to see. If you are in a facility to do benchmarkeing, it is unlikely plant teams will take down all the plant data just for your two or three hour visit. I was in a plant in Germany and we were in an office adjacent to the plant's development center. While in that office, we were told our team was not allowed to enter the development center. However, as our tour guide talked, I noticed that a complete layout of the development center was on the wall including the type and brand of the equipment that was in the center. Since we made sure one of our team members could read German, we effectively found out what new manufacturing technology they were developing without ever seeing the development center.

In another visit to a plant in northern France, I noted all the plant statistics were posted on a wall next to the rest rooms. As we waited for our tour guide and some members of the benchmarking team who were in the rest room, I was able to jot down the plants reject rate, daily volume, machine uptime, ongoing process capability and could identify which products had the highest volume. It took 5 minutes to read the wall and I did not understand French—numbers and statistical process control techniques are a common language throughout most of the industrial world.

'Trick Three' is a lesson I learned from numerous benchmarking trips that relates to how you finish your benchmarking day. This is probably the hardest thing to do after a long day but becomes the most productive part of the day. The trick here is to get your team to meet in the evening following what is usually a very intense day. You need to compare notes and get agreement on what each member of the team saw. Even though each member might have written down all that they observed, it will be surprising, when re-capping, that there will be a lot of information picked up by each individual in the form of a mental snapshot of the plant and its processes. These mental snapshots are still fresh in a persons mind following the visit but will subside very fast. There is a lot of good data in these mental snap-shops which you can't afford to loose. Meeting in the evening for the purpose of dragging out this hidden data and getting it on paper is a very hard discipline to enforce on your benchmarking team after a 10 to 12 hour day. It usually takes a very intense discussion followed by note taking. As the saying goes, a picture is worth a 1000 words. During a plant visit, the benchmarking team will mentally absorb thousands of snapshots in their mind and unless that information is put on paper before day's end, most of the data will be lost.

'Trick four', the final part of benchmarking, is to measure your success and the quality of the information you received. Usually when you visit a competitor's facility, you only get a few hours in their facility. However, you will be surprised how much information you are able to extract. Much of the data will be soft. In other words, the information will not necessarily be in a form that can be applied into some metric. It could be in a form that you can only verbalize such as their motivation to develop new technologies, creative plant operating schemes, quality efforts, vertical integration, etc. This is valuable and most often more important than the hard financial metrics. So 'Trick Four' is to make sure you verbalize and write down what your team concludes are some of the soft observations from your benchmarking. For instance: your competitor may have directionally lower costs but his engineering specifications may be much looser, or he has access to lower cost labor, or is on a site in a state or country that does not require the same health and safety investments, etc. Directionally you must identify the issues, some of which you may be able to do something about, and others not. Whatever the results, the benchmarking study is not complete until you developed an action plan and implement a system to monitor progress to that plan—'Trick Five'.

EP's Story Part #3—Benchmarking

Having developed a plan for a skunk works and a concept to sell their design for manufacture, EP has to get going on developing the technology and establishing the needed design rules. However, the engineering team needs to become a lot more knowledgeable on this new technology and learn whatever they can from available resources.

DG asked for a one on one meeting with Dennis. He said, "you got everybody on the team excited about our future—but you need to understand, neither I nor any of my team know very much about this technology and we don't really know if the technology is ready to apply into a capable manufacturing process."

Dennis responded, "I suspected you would be in here with that comment. I know your team is strung out on day to day items and can't keep abreast of new developments. But what you are going to have to do is take a time out from your routine and benchmark some other companies and industries. You have to get smart real fast. After the last meeting, I told Mary that we were probably going to overrun the travel budget this year since I will need to send you and some other members of EP out on benchmarking trips."

DG rolled his eyes and said, "well, I guess you are ahead of me and I better start moving."

"I suspect you thought about this for a few minutes before you came into my office," said Dennis. "What do you think should be the approach? Who do you recommend visiting?"

DG had already been thinking about this before he came into Dennis' office. He handed Dennis a little Q&A that he jotted down in order to get his thoughts on paper. It highlighted three points.

- *Do we visit other Toy Manufacturers? No. EP is looking for molding and electronic manufacturing technology and processes.*

- *Do we visit molders who also do some form of assembly? Yes. We should pick companies that mold small parts since that is the size of the products EP makes and size will dictate the type of facilities the benchmarked company utilize. Whether those companies assemble molded parts with electronic components or not is a secondary issue. The assembly technique is the item of interest to EP.*

- *Do we visit a Silicon Valley type of company? Yes. We want to find out what is going on in electronic circuit board manufacturing and even if we visit a company that makes supercomputers or missile packages, there is something to be learned.*

After reading the list, Dennis said, "this is good start. But I want you to remember that whenever you visit another facility, you get ideas. A good benchmarking trip will help to clarify your objectives. But you must make sure that just because someone else is doing things a certain way, that does not mean it is necessarily better than EP's processes. You have to be careful of what you see and if it is relevant.

Several years ago, I chaired a benchmarking team that that was looking at the manufacturing of air conditioning compressors. During our first trip to the plant that our team benchmarked, we saw the highlights but not a lot of detail. However, we learned enough to realize that we needed to get more information. Following that trip, my company signed a technology sharing agreement on product design. Additionally, the agreement gave us access to all of our competitor's facilities. Therefore, as a follow-up, five of us went on a second benchmarking team trip. As happened during the first trip, we walked by one of the buildings that we did not see during the first trip and our host repeated that we were not cleared for access to this building. However, this time we knew we were suppose to have access to all the buildings so two of us insisted on seeing the mystery building. To our surprise, what we found in this mystery building was not the latest in manufacturing and product technology, but an antiquated manufacturing system that looked like a plant out of the first industrial revolution. I was in that building for only ten minutes and did not need to take down any information. However, here was a prime example of how a quick snapshot engraved on one's mind can mean so much. This company obviously was nowhere near as advanced as we had been led to believe and we started to wonder if we in fact were not as far behind as we had previously thought.

When we re-capped what we saw at the end of the day with the rest of the team, our discussion led us to one major concern: did we really gain anything with our technology agreement or did we give this oversees competitor an open door to view our technology? Of more concern was the thought that we should not have signed a reciprocal information sharing agreements.

Make sure that you tell your benchmarking team that other companies have paradigms and they may do things because that's the way they always have done them. A competitor or someone doing similar manufacturing may have to operate under different circumstances. That makes their decision matrix different. You will never have enough time in any plant you visit to understand all those details that go into their respective decision matrix, but you can get a good start."

"I get it," said DG.

"Okay," said Dennis, *"now that I got my little sermon out of the way on my experiences benchmarking, who do you suggest should be on EP's benchmarking team?"*

DG thought about and than said, *"beyond 4 or 5 people will make the team unwieldy and we will loose effectiveness. Also, I get nervous when too many outsiders come into our plant since you can't keep your eye on them; I assume other companies also get nervous if too many people show up. We therefore will limit the team to five at most. Also, we may change team members depending on which type of facility we will visit. I think we will obviously require a diverse background group of individuals. My thoughts are that the base team should include a financial analyst, an industrial engineer, a process engineer and a production or floor type. The team leader should be a manager. The manager who will get stuck implementing this technology."*

"That sounds like you," said Dennis. *Care to argue the point?"*

DG just gave Dennis one of those why did I come in here looks. *"Moving on,"* DG said, *"alternate team members would be someone from human resources and product design but that would make the team too large so I recommend we stick with the five members I identified. Of course,"* said DG, *"we can always eliminate the manager?"*

Dennis responded. *"Nice try, but you're going. You have the monkey on your back on this one. Besides, a benchmarking team needs someone with a title to get into the right doors. Status talks to status. Four of the team members will do the detail work and you, having a manager title, will handle the political part of the visit. Also, since you're the manager that will have to implement this technology, you're the one who will benefit most from the findings. That way the team will have a very clear direction and will be results oriented."*

"Since you put it that way," said DG, *"I volunteer. I will meet with the other mangers and we will pick the team and some local companies we should visit and—"*

Dennis stopped DG, saying, *"hold on, you're going a little fast. You have to think about whom it is you want to benchmark. There is no free lunch. If a company allows you to come in and visit their plant, then they expect the same. Since EP is a U.S. based operation, you may want to pick a couple of European plants. This will keep you away from local competitor, that is, from the molding end of the business. For the electronics side, I want the team to go to the hi-tech corridors and find the latest in electronic circuit manufacture. Here you may try to arrange a visit with someone like Intel or Motorola. But since we are not really a pure electronics house, it will be necessary to do a little digging and find companies that are moving along the lines of development that interest us. The auto industry, computer industry and consumer electronics appear to be the areas of most advancement. However, we are in the toy business so we want to stay away from toy companies less we tip our hand on what we are thinking. So maybe you better get some leads before you pick the plants and companies you want to benchmark."*

"You know where we ought to go to get leads?" said DG.

"Where?" Asked Dennis.

"The best two places to go in order to get leads on who appears to be ahead of the game in molding and electronics are the "K" Show in Dusseldorf, Germany and the Consumer Electronics Show in Las Vegas. The "K" show is held every three years and is the largest plastics show in the world. Anyone who is anyone in plastic materials or processing go to that show. The show happens to be this year. We can send our benchmarking team to the show and find out who is buying the latest equipment. Additionally, the industry material and facility suppliers are usually the ones that have contacts and can get us into the manufacturers we are interested in seeing. Barb can get her suppliers to give us some contacts at the "K" show. From the electronics end, the yearly Las Vegas Consumer Electronics show is the place to go to talk to manufacturers and get leads on who is doing what."

Dennis concurred and told DG to visit the technology shows prior to the benchmarking trips. "I think that is enough discussion on this subject for now," Dennis said.

With that, DG departed to get his team together.

Armed with leads from these two industry shows, EP developed a list of companies they wanted to visit. They wrote letters to the contacts made at those shows and asked to arrange visits. EP also gave them a detailed list of the agenda items and areas of interest. Each plant visit would be arranged through the engineering departments if possible. Experience has shown you always want to try and arrange visits through the engineering community. Why? Normally the engineers not only know about plant level details, but engineers by nature are proud of what they do and want to share it with whoever will listen. So engineers are always the best of source of company data. They have trouble keeping their mouth shut to put it bluntly.

With confirmation on their visits and the benchmarking trip set, DG called his team together to get organized. "First thing we need to do," said DG, is to benchmark our own plant. We need to know every detail on our plant's processes, products and cost structure. You may think you do now, but I guarantee you that you don't. Jot down the same information about EP's operating systems that you expect to get from the benchmarking trip. Put it down into a form that we will carry with us on the trip. That way as we walk through a competitor's plant, we will have a list of key areas of interest we want to prioritize. The information or data we observe can they be noted on a sheet of paper which has our own internal procedures written down. In this way, we will automatically highlight any significant differences. If we see a significant difference and it is not obvious, we can do a deeper dive on the spot."

George, the industrial engineer on team commented, "since each of us will have different pieces of information, someone better consolidate all the data and–"

"Thanks for volunteering," said DGs. "You're the consolidator."

George did not comment.

DG continued. "Don't worry, George, every one of the team members will get an assignment. Now, let's move forward. Since our team will have precious little time when we are at the facility to be benchmarked, each of you will have an area to concentrate on during the plant tours and conference room debriefing sessions. George, since you are the industrial engineer, your assignment when we are on the plant tour is to count heads for each manufacturing process operation. Count the people directly related to running a machine. Additionally, try to categorize the individuals in the area of the machine being addressed as to the type of function they perform.

"Judy is our financial analyst in case any one hasn't guessed," continued DG. "During the plant tour, Judy, you are going to have to do some of the functions George normally performs as an industrial engineer. Not your normal function, but I need to split up the data gathering process if we are to get as much information as possible."

"Okay," said Judy. "What do I do?"

DG responded. "I want you to bring a stop watch and if you don't have one I am sure George does. You will time the machine cycles. The cycle being the total time it takes to run one part through each process step being viewed."

"I understand," said Judy. "From the two pieces of information, the number of people in the process which George will get and the amount of time it takes to make a part which I will get from my stop watch, we can calculate the work standard or number of minutes to make a part. And if someone can find out the labor rate, George and I can do the math and get the labor cost per piece."

"Plus," said George, "if someone on the team can count the non direct labor (labor which is not directly related to making the part such as fork lift truck drivers, quality control inspections and material handlers), we can get a feel for the burden rate that each part has to absorb."

DG jumped into the conversation and said, "now you're getting the idea. I will try and get the non-direct labor headcount. As we walk through the plant I should be able to observe some of the key support labor. But since I will be with our tour guide, I can hopefully supplement that with questions which, taken out of context, should not be too threatening to our tour guide. I am sure he or she will answer some of my questions. At least enough to get most of the information."

"What does Norm, our trusty process engineer do while the rest of the team is counting heads and checking cycle times?" Asked Judy.

"That should be obvious," said DG. "While the rest of us are counting heads and taking times, Norm will be looking at the construction of the tools, the degree of automation built into the tools, how much automation is on the equipment, and how the process is set up. Norm needs to make a gut call, in a very few minutes as we walk by a process, as to what decisions might have been made when the local processing people decided on the degree of automation."

Looking puzzled, Mary wondered, "why is that important?"

"Obviously your not a plant person," said Norm. "Let me tell you a little story. I once saw a highly automated lighting manufacture in Germany that molded lamp bodies and dumped them into a very expensive walking beam conveyor. At the end of the line the parts were dumped hap-hazardly into a box. They could have acquired a much cheaper belt conveyer for a fraction of the cost of a walking beam conveyor. My only conclusion was that this was Germany, and Germans love automation. It was gorgeous if you were an engineer who liked neat equipment, but totally unnecessary."

"So you see," said DG. "It was a gut decision on Norm's part. Norm was benchmarking and only had time to make one of two decisions—either this was the way to process a job or it wasn't."

Judy smiled thinking it really was a dumb question now that she thought about it.

"What about Harry?" Said Norm, "our representative from production."

"I'll do anything," said Harry. "I haven't been off EP's production floor for ten years. I will go anyplace, anytime, at the company's expense. So what is my assignment, DG?"

You are the team member that will look at the supervision on the floor, who reports to who, and how the floor structure works, "said DG. "I want you to ask questions like:

- *Do the maintenance people report to a central maintenance organization or the area production supervision?*

- *Does the plant inspect in quality, generally known as quality inspection or do they quality control through statistical process control?*

- *Are the production operators relieved during the day? Do they get a break and if they do does the plant have relief operators?*

Your most important function, however," said DG, "is to read everything that is written on the machines and on whatever boards are posted in the plant. Most manufacturing operations will have boards mounted near the production line with charts on them that will tell someone more about a plant operation than a annual report.

Quality levels, production rates, downtime and miscellaneous other plant information that could indicate a lot about the plant's culture could be found here."

"Overtime schedules could also be posted," said Norm.

"Which leads me another thought," said DG. "Once we enter the plant gate, all eyes should be on anything that is posted on the walls of the plant or the building. Especially as we walk through the office areas to get into the plant. It will be everyone's assignment to read what is on the walls."

Judy noted at that point, "I don't think I will be able to write down what I see as I am walking through office areas."

"No you can't," said DG, "and I don't expect you to. But you've heard the phrase, a picture is worth a 1000 words. I want each team member to take a mental snapshot of what they see. At the end of our day, we are going to have dinner and then get together, probably in a good bar—over a beer or two—and we will try and take each of our mental pictures and put them into words. You will find each of us saw the same thing but our minds registered different aspects of what we saw. I want to piece that information together and hopefully we will get a good overall idea of what we all saw in a brief passing."

"DG, you said your function was to look at the indirect labor while you're keeping the tour guide busy," said Norm. "What else do you think you can get out of him?"

"That is a good question and I should comment on it," said DG. "There is a lot of other information we need to know to get a feel for the cost structure of the products and processes we are looking at—for instance:

- How many holidays does the plant have?

- Does the plant have a higher pay scale for off shift operations?

- Is there overtime?

- What is the average work week?

- How do they decide on capacity?

- Where do parts get shipped to and how do they get there?

- What are the fringe benefits and what does the plant define as a fringe benefit?

"Why are these important to us?" Asked Harry. "Whatever they are it doesn't affect us and we probably can't do anything about our situation in these areas anyway."

Judy agreed with Harry's comment.

DG said, *"you are not thinking this through. All the items I mentioned above affect how the plant makes decisions on its processes, where the plant is located and on and on. We need to understand all of this detail if we are to properly interpret the information we get. Let me give you some examples. In Germany, the average work-week is usually 36 hours. Overtime is limited and women can not work the off shifts without special approval. In Mexico, employees get a free lunch as part of the company's perks. And it is usually very good lunch and tends to be the main meal for the workers. Japan includes housing and many companies have dormitories or housing similar to married housing on a university campus. These perks are part of company compensation packages in those countries. They have a cost that you need to know if you want to get at the cost structure for the product they produce. I once benchmarked a company in Spain that did not have any incremental employees to cover absentee-ism—whether vacation, AWOLs, or medical leaves. They would just call the local employment office each morning and request the added number of individuals needed for the day to run the production requirements. This, of course, is just the opposite of most American companies, who keep extra employees on the payroll to cover absentee-ism. This little piece of information could be the root cause of a plant's decision to use heavy automation or to go with a more manual process. That is why this data is criti-cal to know."*

"And speaking of automation, that is the next and last subject of our discussion. It is critical," said DG, *"that our little team get a feel for the philosophy towards auto-mation at the plants visited. There is a catch to buying automation. A point exists where emergency downtime and normal maintenance make automation unproduc-tive. The degree depends on the industry, plant, and local work rules. In my last job,"* said DG, *"I benchmarked a highly automated plant that makes large fuel tanks in Germany. On the surface the automation was impressive and one not knowledgeable about the specifics of the process details would be amazed at the system they installed. I counted the employees assigned to the process and the cycle time and came up with numbers equivalent to what we had seen in a non-automated plant the day before. Confused, I asked the question at the exit meeting as to why they spent so much money on automation. I expected some scripted comment but instead was shocked when they said the amount of automation didn't pay out as predicted and they would never do it again. In fact, they said they were building a new plant in another country and it would be heavily de-automated. I tell you, had our benchmarking team not done all the things I just discussed with you which led to the question I asked, we may have gone off and concluded this was a wave of the future and made the same mistake. The other thing that surprised me was that even in Germany, where labor rates were the highest in the world at that time, automation had its limits."*

"All it takes is one observation to affect everything you may be planning on doing and that is where benchmarking becomes so important." said DG. "It is not the quantity of the information that is important, but it is those one or two little things that will make the difference. A few years ago I was in a plant in Colgne, Germany and had stopped to see an old friend. He gave me a quick plant tour to show me where he worked. As I was walking through the plant, I saw a robot hanging upside down from the ceiling. The processing opportunities were immediately obvious to me. My mindset had always been, you have to mount a robot on the floor as robots are seen as a replacement for human being. However, there is no reason why you can't run them upside down. That one observation yielded major productivity improvements in the plant I was working in and the floor space savings eliminated the need for a building expansion. It may sound obvious when I talk about it, but each of us has developed paradigms and you can only break them by observing how other people do things. So, that is why, when we return, we will have to write up everything we have seen.

Judy, you will have to work with George on the financials. Harry, you will write you thoughts on a different way to run the floor operations. And Norm, you and I will put our heads together on all the new processes and manufacturing technology we saw and get back to Dennis and his operating team with our conclusions and recommendations."

Judy asked, "like what kind of recommendations do you expect?"

"That is easy," said DG. "The main conclusion is whether we continue to go forward with our business strategy and bring in this new technology or forget about it and stop development in the skunk works."

"If you do that," said Harry, "we won't have a future and based on what I have been told, we could be out of business in the next five years."

DG smiled and let that comment sit for a few minutes. He finally said, "you get the picture. If the cost of the technology and the estimated cost to manufacture, which Judy will work out, is to high to be viable for our customer, then we don't have a future. Would our customer buy a $50 part from us if he can only get $30 for the end item from the customer? Of course not—and if that is the way this turns out, our business plan is no good."

"I understand," said Harry. "Now I know why this little trip and all this detailed effort is a lot more critical than what I had first thought."

Take Away Thoughts

Benchmarking doesn't always give you the answers and may just confuse you more. The reason benchmarking becomes so important for the manufacturing person is the discipline you must follow will make you realize that you never truly understood your own system. And if you don't understand your own system, you will not be able to follow the first two experience principals. What is important is to remember benchmarking must be dynamic—it never stops. You are always looking at data at a point in time. Your competitors may be doing the same thing you are—trying to figure out where you are going. And it could be to a technology place where you already were. It is a natural tendency to think someone else knows more than you know.

- Benchmark your own process first.

- Benchmark other industries that may have similar processes.

- More data can be obtained from a company that is not a direct competitor.

- Pick you team from all disciplines. No two from the same discipline.

- What you don't find is just as important as what you do find. Note it.

- Benchmark a plant that is not perceived as state of the art. You may be closer to them than you think.

- Always benchmark several facilities on the same trip. It gives you perspective.

- Read the walls. All real data in a plant can be found on walls, and machines.

- Always end the day with a re-cap meeting. Note all visual observations.

- Develop an action plan to follow-up on your major observations.

- The soft information, knowledge that does not have a direct metric, can be the biggest find from a benchmarking trip.

Experience Principle #4:
Identify the Customers Itch and Scratch It

What is a customer itch? Generally. an itch is quality related when it comes to manufacturing, but it could be anything. An "itch", or a customer irritation usually is one of the following;

- A want for a product or feature;
- Wanting improved productivity from a supply or process;
- A quality issue;
- Logistics issues;
- Not meeting performance objectives;
- Not responsive to marketing and sales changes;
- Design shortfalls that affect manufacturing.

Many of the above issues or "itches" may not be your problem to resolve. However, in manufacturing anything relating to the supply chain of a product usually ends up as a plant problem. So you must react. Putting effort into blaming some other function doesn't help to improve a plant's image—fixing problems does.

If your customer has an "itch" and expects your operation to resolve it, you will usually find that you are in the "trick bag" without an immediate or long term solution. However, once they believe you are addressing the concern, it satisfies them even if the problem is not solved immediately—or is never fully resolved. Being up-front with a customer and taking responsibility to address one of their issues effectively scratches their "itch". The attention and understanding that your give the customer is key. Assuring them that there is a plan and progress to that plan is the important thing.

Who Is the Customer

Ask yourself and the other members of your operating team who they think the customer is and what they perceive to be the customers expectations. If you don't get several different answers, then your team hasn't given it enough thought. You should find that in the world of manufacturing you have several customers. The companies or individuals that purchase your product are only one customer. There are internal customers and external customers. There is a customer chain. If you haven't yet answered the question to who your customer is, here are a few hints:

- Finance—the people who plan, track and bin costs

- Human Resources—the people who find resources

- Research and Development—any project that is not yet planned

- Product Design—programs approved and in the process of affecting your plant

- Engineering—those that direct the design function

- Procurement/Supply—more recently known as logistics; traffic, material control, shipping, materials purchasing

- Marketing—those who develop the strategy for selling your product

- Sales—the individuals who sell your product and may or may not know much about the details

- Aftermarket Sales—known as factory seconds such as items sold at an outlet center

- The Ultimate User—the person who ends up buying your product and using it

- The Recycler—the company that buys your product from the user at the end of its useful life (junk yards, second hand stores, etc)

The answer to who the customer is can be stated as just about everybody. Notice that the ultimate user, the person or company who buys your manufactured service, is only one of a manufacturing plants customer. It should be the most important. However, the bigger your parent organization, the greater the probability that the internal customers will take up more of your time. This, of course, gets back to the concept that to be successful in manufacturing you must be able to handle the gamesmanship. Your objective is to listen to voices of all these customers, identify the customers "itch" (what is bugging him about your product or service), and then develop a value delivery system that scratches that itch.

Whoever the customer is, you must understand that they all are the important to your success. Each one may have a different perception of your product, the service they expect and hidden agendas when it comes to expectations. You must not only understand those perceptions and hidden agendas, but you must also accept the realities of whatever it is the customer wants. These wants can be very contrary to your mindset.

How Do You Identify an Itch.

There are several ways that information can be obtained. Surveys can be taken, field representatives can be utilized, or outside marketing firms are usually available that may feed you the information. What a manufacturing team must realize is that it is not possible to work in a facility and not get sensitized to little nuances in the business. These little nuances can be your perception of acceptable quality or delivery performance that may be totally different from your customer's perception.

Identifying an "itch" may be easy, but addressing it may not be. There are competing values, needs and expectations for each customer. For example: the engineering department may want to manufacture products from predictable highly purified materials. These are materials usually referred to as virgin. Virgin materials predictably will improve (reduce variation) in the quality of products. Simultaneously, environmentalists are pressuring to use recycled materials. Recycled materials are not as predictable and their pedigree can not always be assured. What do you do—how do you listen to the needs of each of these two customers and scratch the root cause of their respective "itches". The answer, of course, is you must be customer focused and address their competing values and still meet the ultimate customer's expectations for quality, cost, and delivery. Not easy is it. In this, the answer might be a compromise such as using materials which have a percentage of post consumer recycled product mixed in with virgin material. A compromise may be the best solution. That is why you must identify each customer and identify their concerns and discuss with your team what your definition of customer focus means. You must get close to the customer. But how?

First and foremost you need feedback. Working in a manufacturing environment you must still identify and address the customers needs through some shorthand approach. Usually you do not have the time for the detailed analysis that a staff function could perform. Even if you have a staff function for this, you need to do some of it on your own as with all things in manufacturing, you need to keep your hands on the pulse of your business. A good shorthand approach was noted in the Harvard Business Review in the late 80's and is still true. These are questions you first ask yourself and then ask the customer through some type of survey:

- Are we easy to do business with?
- Easy to contact?
- Fast to provide information?
- Easy to order from?
- Do we keep promises?
- Follow up on quality improvements?
- Meet customer's delivery timing?
- Train our customer contact people?
- Service the customer?
- Do we meet the standards we set for our business?
- Get specifics about concerns?
- Transmit a supportive general Tone?
- Are we responsive?
- Do we listen?
- Do we follow up?

- Do we have a disciplined approach to identifying root cause and verifying fixes?

- Do we treat customers as individuals?

- Do we work together?

- Share blame?

- Share information?

- Make joint decisions?

- Provide satisfaction?

Answer these questions and you will be able to put together a framework for customer service and needs. Many of these questions, however, can't be answered with some type of metric. I find it best in manufacturing to develop your own metrics. Surveys like satisfied, completely satisfied, etc. help. Many times a numbered evaluation sent out over a certain time period, such as quarterly, will give you an indication. But these numbered evaluations should also include some type of verbatim. Getting feedback through a customer verbatim, which means in a customer's exact words, is an approach I find very useful. In one of my previous functions, I identified an employee who had good phone skills and a pleasing voice. I assigned her to spend most of her day calling customers to get input on warranty claims and service calls. She found that if she could get to a customer within two weeks of their complaint, the individual who complained would remember the details. It was amazing how the information was filtered through the normal quality system channels. Valuable information was lost if follow-up on complaints occurred much beyond a few weeks. Information necessary to developing a solution gets filtered over time and the critical data that is needed to identify the root cause of an issue (itch) may be lost.

Identify the Root Cause of the Itch.

Once you define who the customer is you will need an approach to find out what is really getting to that customer and causing the itch. A good plan is to break down your required actions into a process outline or sequence similar to writing a computer program. You will need a process plan for each customer you have identified as key to your future success.

- First you want to identify the most important information you need to know about a customer. In-depth customer knowledge is critical. You want to know as much about him and his business as the customer does.

- The second item in your process is to build a collaborative relationship and that means that you may have to benchmark some of your customers other suppliers and/or individuals in whom he seems to have confidence. Make sure you understand that there is a difference between a consultative relationship and a partnership. You want his trust therefore you will need to identify which type of relationship meets his comfort level. This can best be done by pooling all the information you can gather from individuals who have been in contact with the customer and what worked and what didn't work with the customer.

- Third, you must identify the customer's needs and wants. There is a difference between needs and wants. Discriminate between the two. You can't offer solutions to the customer itch until you know and understand the problem and if it is a need or a want. Probing questions plus reviewing public information will help to get to the root cause of an "itch".

- The fourth box in your process sheet is to identify the players in the customer's chain and who in your chan needs to face off with the customer. At this point, you want to anticipate the probability of acceptance of your solution which will vary depending on the individuals involved. These customer's acceptance chain varies dramatically from issue to issue and plant to plant. I have seen quality issues where a plant manager has the final say and in one of its sister plants the quality control inspector makes the final call. Same company, different plants and of course, different cultures. You need to understand who has what authority and it usually is not the highest person on the management team totem pole.

- Finally, the fifth step in the process is to develop a solution matrix with clear responsibilities and timing. The process must be monitored continuously and there must be an ongoing flow of information back to the customer on the progress of the solution. A customer's "itch" can usually be satisfied by understanding what it is, what caused it, and driving for a solution. This is the process by which you scratch the itch and the outcome is a happy customer even if it reoccurs and needs a little more scratching.

EP's Story Part #4—Identify the Customer's Itch

Vito, EP's quality supervisor dropped a bomb in the plant staff meeting when he said the plant had a major issue brewing with it's customer. He said, "we better figure out what it is and scratch the itch just as soon as we can before it gets blown out of proportion."

"So what is the problem?" Asked Dennis.

"EP is getting negative feedback from our customer, the toy group, that the plant's sub-assemblies we supply to the toy division are failing prematurely. It is starting to affect the company's market share and they are considering pulling some of the products off the shelf."

"Define premature," said Mary.

"Prematurely," said Vito, "is defined as earlier than historic and industry acceptable durability levels. So we are going to have to get to the root cause of the problem before we can go any further."

"It could be the design," said DG. "However, whatever the root cause, it appears that this is our issue (itch) to resolve. So we need to go through our own discovery process. Vito—you need to find out ASAP if market share loss is an excuse—do all toys in this same category have similar useful lives, or is EP's different?"

"Be careful how you do that," said Dennis. "Terminology is critical when you try to define root cause. Let me give an example. An automotive parts supplier I was working with early in my career was being inundated with field complaints on weather strip performance—a product we made and supplied. The complaints were being downloaded via a time consuming warranty reporting system. Using the field data supplied, million of dollars were spent in development of a solution over an extended period of time while complaints persisted—this time lag just made the itch worse. When the new product was introduced to solve the perceived problem, however, nothing changed. The problem persisted.

It was at this point that we decided it was time to talk directly with the customer. That is, we started contacting customers directly as opposed to waiting to get the information through the system that was developed by the quality office. It did not take many phone calls before it became obvious that the customer's understanding of what they defined as weather strip did not jive with what the industry called weather strip. In the customer's vernacular, they had problems with what the industry called body side molding. Customers thought body side molding was called weather strip. Weather strip in industry vernacular is the part on a car that goes around the door frame to seal the doors from wind noise and rain when the doors are closed. My plant, which manufactured the weather strip, not only tried to improve on a part that was not broken but also tried to address a problem on a part they did not make. What was worse, we got a poor supplier reputation and were on the verge of losing future business. The message I wanted to give you is that if you attempt to scratch an itch but scratched the wrong itch, it can be worse than doing nothing. So make sure you are asking the right questions and everyone has the same definition."

With that assignment in hand, Vito did not stay for the rest of the plant meeting and left to get started. During the investigation, Vito found design flaws in EP's products—flaws their competitors did not have. He determined that there was a unique problem with EP's product but the root cause was in the design. The plant's problem, however, was that their customer, the toy operation, did not know the cause of the problem nor did they care—they just wanted it fixed. As is normal, the assembly operations were the one's getting the heat from marketing since they were the last ones in the manufacturing chain.

As is also typical, designers claim field issues are manufacturing defects. They usually note that the design meet the system engineering specifications so it could not possibly be a design issue. Of course they are the same ones that developed the test specifications—specifications which may not be relevant to field performance. This mindset must be considered when EP picks the approach needed to resolve the problem.

With the itch now identified, Vito headed for Dennis' office to discuss next steps.

Reading Vito's analysis, Dennis started to think out loud. "What we need to do is build confidence with both parties. Since we need to get trust, I don't think a consultative relationship will work. We are not designers but manufacturers. I have to accept the fact that being in manufacturing even if some of our people have doctorates in engineering, we will be perceived as not capable of identifying a design issue and will be ignored if we point the finger at design. So you can not solve the issue by using a consultative approach. Therefore we must collaborate and not try to fix blame."

"Also, there is definitely a need, not a want, to solve this problem as it is affecting market share. The final assembler, our customer, is getting the blame and he is blaming EP. Since he does not have in-house engineering capability to solve the issue, the only thing he can do is yell, scream and point fingers at us."

Dennis continued. "What you and DG need to do is meet with the product engineering community and suggest that the solution could be a design for manufacture approach. Tell them you concluded that EP's manufacturing process is not sufficiently robust to manufacture the current design and that there might be a possible alternative. This will keep the design group from taking an offensive position and hopefully they will support our efforts."

"One other thing," said Dennis, "I suggest using a disciplined approach to problem solving. Problems do not get resolved unless you write them down in some sort of disciplined fashion. And, using a disciplined approach is about the best method there is to show our customer we have a plan and status towards a solution. This should prove that we have gone through the mental gymnastics to address the issue—it will scratch their itch."

"I think I know what you mean," said Vito. "But why not go over it so there is no misunderstanding."

"Good idea," said Dennis. "Here is what I mean by a disciplined approach to solving an "itch". And this means everything is written down. That is the key to the discipline. There are seven disciplines:

Discipline One: establish a cross functional team. Your team should include plant manufacturing engineering people, the product design folks, a production/floor type of supervisor who will be the person accountable to implement the change and someone from material logistics.

Discipline Two: describe the problem. The problem is that our product is failing prematurely. However, we do not know why it is failing or what is failing. So the team needs to use all the information at hand to try and describe the problem. Any statistical information that can be had should be included. Since we want to be able to measure our success, we need to identify the failure rate and how, when and under what circumstances it might occur.

Discipline Three: define the root cause of the problem. How did it occur? Also, at this point you will have to address how the problem escaped from your plant. If there was a design flaw and it was not caught in the plant, then it follows that there must be a flaw in the process inspection, testing or certification process. So it looks like we may have two root cause paths.

Discipline Four: develop interim corrective actions. How can we contain the problem from getting out of the plant until there is a permanent bullet proof solution.

Discipline Five: implement the corrective actions. Here it gets a little tricky. Using a collaborative approach, Vito and DG will suggest that the root cause of the issue is that we have major problems manufacturing the part and it would help if we had a more robust design for manufacture. In other words, you do not attack the design, but suggest that the process would be more robust if they, product engineering, would agree *to make some design adjustments. Assuming agreement by the team and the fix is implemented, you can then move forward and go to the next step.*

Discipline Six: verify the effectiveness of the fix. Here is where you get more statistics, plot data, etc. and compare it against the data collection in step two. There is always a tendency not to verify results as by the time you get to this level, individuals in the team are usually involved in some other disaster. In manufacturing these days, there's always a disaster or two in the mill.

Discipline Seven: prevent similar issues from happening again. Why did the above problem happen, and how can we prevent a similar problem from developing on a like part or process? In EP's case, they concluded a more robust design for manufacture approach would have caught the problem. DG may want to suggest a team based design analysis system for future products.

However, I am getting ahead of the process and it will be up to your team to implement them and come up with a way to prevent reoccurrence of the problem."

Vito understood and got his team going. He got the designers to agree to make changes in the design to get a more robust manufacturing process. The results were a higher quality output and significant reduction in early mortality failures. Using the statistics generated to verify the fix, the team reported back to the assembly operations on the changes to product and process showing them how they solved the problem.

EP's quality team identified the "itch" and with their ad hoc design for manufacture team approach, generated an ongoing information flow to "scratch the itch". The disciplined write-up was the mechanism used to "scratch the itch". Marketing and sales were sub players, but not key. However, the team still needed to get back to them with the results.

Action plans and an ongoing status towards a solution must be written down and reported on regularly. Not only because it forces the discipline and creates a reporting document, but as Tom Clancy wrote in one of his novels, "if isn't written down it didn't happen." Be assured, the history and fix for the problem will be lost and this means it will happen again—at which time your credibility as a supplier goes down the tube.

Key Take Away Thoughts

Marketing folks have developed systems and processes to identify customers and their needs. A manufacturer's roll is not all that organized. Sometimes there is only one customer and one itch but it can destroy your reputation.

- Identify your customers.

- Find out what "itches" them—what problems are they sensitive about?

- Identify the root cause. Fix or contain the root cause—this will scratch the "itch".

- Develop a disciplined approach to problem solving.

- Communicate the disciplined problem solving approach to the customer.

- Communicate the solution.

- Make sure the sub players, customers not necessarily in the loop, are kept informed.

- Track long term performance to verify the solution to the "itch" is permanent.

As a check and balance to this process, you want to go back to the items listed from the Harvard business school and see if you can't answer yes to all of them. As you will find, it becomes an unending process. If there is a potential "itch" which could surface, you need to get at it as soon as possible with some preventative approach. This is called predictive planning.

Experience Principle #5: Be Technology's Fastest Follower

You have choices. You can have an extensive research and development organization that can choose to:

- spend time and money inventing new technology,
- be a fast follower of technology as it is being developed in your industry and related industries,
- or your can keep to the status quo.

Industrialution is continuously changing the ways of manufacturing so a status quo position is in fact establishing a going out of business plan. The other extreme, having a major research and development organization, is very costly, time consuming, and it generally becomes hard to measure the value of such a group. Adding the overhead costs for an R&D organization will drive most plants to non-competitiveness—unless the developments are able to leapfrog competitors and it is the only way your operation will be able to survive. This leaves the fast follower scenario. Being a fast follower means a plant management has to run at warp speed to keep up with technological changes and in the process try to stay ahead—how far ahead will be discussed later in this chapter. And if this is not enough, you have to recognize technology when you see it.

Do You Know Technology When You See It

Technological developments aren't usually as obvious as the invention of the light bulb, but come in little doses that evolve into a megatrend over time. You need to recognize this happening before the megatrend becomes obvious to all—all being defined as your competitors.

As part of the business element, you must have objectives related to the future viability of your operation. In other words, you have to keep pace with developing technologies. If you do not know where the your industry is going, if you are not at the forefront of developing technologies, then it becomes very difficult to plan out your long term objectives, modernization needs, product changes, etc. At the turn of the century would you have proposed a major facility modernization for manufacturing buggy whips? Or would you have maintained the current facilities? Today the answer is obvious. We wonder if it was that intuitive in the early 1900's.

I had an opportunity to discuss this ability to recognize technology when you see it with a (what people normally refer to as) rocket scientist who worked in an aerospace firm in the Silicon Valley. He was asked to spend a year in a mid-western heavy manufacturing facility with the intent of trying to improve the mindset of the engineers toward developing new technologies. He commented, during one of his discussions, that "there is a more complex set of electronic algorithms and problem scenarios in most electronic toys designed for a 6 year old than there is in a rocket"—he believes toys are truly the most highly engineered product today. His perception was that an automobile is probably next in technical difficulty after toys, followed by aerospace technology. The mid-western manufacturer thought this aerospace engineer could help what they perceived as a non-technical facility. In the end, just the opposite occurred. The scientist took the smoke stack industry engineers back to his aerospace facility expecting they could do more good at his plant than he could do for this supposedly non-technical smoke stack industrial operation. It convinced me that recognizing technology isn't easy or necessarily what people perceive as technology. Real technology, which can give your operation a competitive advantage, is usually found in obscure places and may have been around but not recognized.

I once was given a problem that highlights these concepts. The problem related to finding a reliable way to verify that automotive gas tanks did not leak. For years processes used in most industries for leak testing to certify products free of holes, cracks, etc, used water as the test medium, which was highly unreliable due to its viscous quality. Helium, which was always considered an alternative, worked for high pressure applications. However, gas tanks could only handle very low pressure drops—and no one had been able to make helium work due to the fact that there are trace amounts of helium in normal air. Since helium exists in air, the only way engineers assumed they could use helium as a test medium was to build vacuum chambers. Vacuum chambers are not only unreliable in a manufacturing environment, but costly. Therefore, I gave this problem to one of my engineers and told him to look for a different approach to using helium in an industrial environment. I suggested he look at the difference between helium in the test chamber before and after the test.

His fresh eyes approach resulted in one simple conclusion: if you check the helium content in the air before the test and after and just measure the difference, you can get the leak rate no matter how much the ambient level of helium changes. He also determined that this had to be done very fast to keep up with manufacturing line rates. That would have required a lot of data to be taken and analyzed in seconds—not minutes or hours. Combining his approach with recent developments in factory floor microprocessor technology made helium leak testing possible for a robust industrial test application. He did not invent microprocessors, did not do the work that made them robust on the factory floor, nor did he invent the concept of using helium for leak testing. What he recognized were the elements of these technologies and his development time was extremely fast and with little up front financial requirements. Factory floor microprocessor technology and equipment to identify trace amount of helium in air were major costly developments absorbed by other organizations in other companies. However, they were not part of the overhead costs and R&D structure for our plant. My engineer knew technology when he saw it. This engineer was a fast follower. And it gave the plant a competitive advantage which ended up being part of a technical presentation for new business.

What Is Technology

You must understand what technology you have in your plant, what it really means in your manufacturing environment and how to best capitalize on it for the future. You can not just assume a position that your facility does or doesn't require rocket science engineering. The key to technology in manufacturing is in the details. A new product development may be required to keep your company in business, but for you who live inside a manufacturing plant, what might seem as a minor detail to the outside world could become the breakthrough that keeps you ahead of your competition. You have all heard the phrase we tried it years ago and it didn't work. In today's level of industrialution, technologies that didn't work in previous phases of industrialution may well work today. Manufacturers who tried something new and found it wasn't developed or didn't perform as expected rarely recognize the root cause of why it didn't work. Usually it is some minor development that was not perfected at the time, but was subsequently invented and proven out at a later date.

We tend to assume everyone knows technology when they see it as if it was some intuitively obvious phenomenon. Unfortunately, it is not that simple. So what is technology? In manufacturing, if you don't have a process technology or product technology, than any level of technology that exists outside your operation is new technology. Even if it might have been around in other industries for years. So my definition of technology for manufacturing comes in the form of the three ifs;

- If you don't have it, it is new.
- If it is still to be invented or developed, then it is state of the art.
- If you can optimize a technology to the point of simplicity, then it becomes deactivated technology. Many times what seems to be a very difficult set of options, can be broken down into some simple alternatives such that you can conclude that you no longer need the technology you were developing. This is just as important a breakthrough as a major innovation.

Common sense tells us that whatever your process is, it operates at some technological level of development or what is known as state of the art. Experience tells us that old technologies always deliver more than people expect and new ones always cost more and take longer to get to market than expected. So your team's first objective is to understand its base of manufacturing technology and second, project how far you can stretch the old technologies. Simplifying a process can be a greater technological breakthrough than adding some high tech machine vision systems, robots, or microprocessors.

What Are Your Technology Objectives

Combining you estimate of how far you can take your current in house technology with what you learned in the benchmarking trips, your manufacturing team can decide on which of the following strategies are best for your plant:

- Stay with current equipment and technology and spend your effort on small but consistent productivity improvements?

- Replace current equipment with the latest state of the art?

- Or leapfrog the competitors with a whole new approach and new types of product and processes?

What are your processing and technology objectives? In 1817, David Ricardo proposed the following: "assuming the existence of trade, a country that has an absolute advantage over other countries in the production of everything should nevertheless produce only that in which its relative advantage is greatest while importing that in which its relative advantage is not as great." I have found this concept has not changed over the phases of "Industrialuion" and can be applied to a manufacturing operation. Ricardo's law, when correlated to individual manufacturing operations, can be stated: assuming the existence of a market for your product, a manufacturing plant that has an absolute advantage over other competitors in the production of that product should nevertheless manufacture that in which its relative advantage is greatest (namely a technology advantage) while purchasing the service and/or parts in which its relative advantage is not as great. In other words, spend your time and money on technology followership that gives you an advantage. Relegate the things your operation does not do well to outside suppliers or resources as those technologies or services may be a commodity product when looked at independently and offer no value advantage to you. You do not want to spend your valuable resources in a non-valued area.

You expect that your Board of Directors has a technology roadmap for the company at large. In turn, they expect you are doing the same thing within the four walls of your manufacturing facility. However, in the current world the concept of protecting a plants future through new developments or invention of new technology is being strained more than it ever has been in the previous phases of "Industrialution". One of the key aspects of "Industrialution" which we are going through, can best be described as the "Jack Welch" phase named after the long term CEO and spiritual leader of that group of CEOs who are proponents of his philosophy on how to run companies. A synopsis of this group's philosophy can best be stated as *instant gratification to the stock holders and a great rate of return or get out of the business. Be first, second in your industry or don't play.* General Electric has been very successful under this philosophy so you can't fault it nor do you want to. What you want to do is understand that it has to be part of the game plan for your plant. Be first or second in manufacturing technology globally—it is what should drive your fast follower strategy.

One thing about manufacturing is that there is always one objective that is usually straightforward: get a quality product out the door on time. But in any company, there are usually other objectives which may written or unwritten (hidden agenda) and part of the corporate culture. These are the objectives you must understand. They become part of the game. Any good plant operating team will know how to "milk a plant". Simply stated this means you can optimize your performance today at the expense of future year performance. If your objective is to look good today assuming you will not be around tomorrow, technology objectives will not be necessary. However, the premise of this book is that this is not an acceptable position to assure a plant has a future.

Fast Follower Timing

Planners generally operate around five year plans. In the world today, if you get to be two years ahead of the competition, you are in "tall clover" as the saying goes. Many companies have strategic planning units. You must also have a planning unit for your plant. except in your case, the operating team doubles as the planning unit. The plant planning unity does not have to be sophisticated. It does not have to put together those neat looking marking/business plans that companies do when they want to go public on the stock market. All you want to do is know enough to, as we discussed earlier, stay two years ahead of the competition and that plan should only take one sheet of paper—or you don't understand your plan. Buying equipment for the new technologies means you're usually 24 months ahead of production startup and 12 months ahead implementing the processes. It is at this 24 month out period that a plant operating team (the same individuals who must get day to day production out the door) should be meeting regularly to plot the course of the plant and the technologies that must be launched. This becomes one of the hardest things for a plant team to focus on since you are not there to be strategic planners, but there to produce (add value to whatever commodity you manufacture). However, in the process of making a product while simultaneously attempting to maintain the cost structure, you are in the best position to get the feel for the pulse of the facility. A manufacturing team in a plan has an understanding of what is doable and what becomes difficult to do with the paradigms that exist in any organization. To do this, you must have a strategy that requires that you're always meeting, discussing and planning for technologies out for the next three years. With a three-year plan, you have the luxury of adjusting the third year. The plan automatically becomes the plan as it gets cast in stone two years out. With the built in inertia to change a major facility and reeducate the human resources (people need to be trained which usually requires a mindset to change their built in paradigms), you find that you are locked into your plans for the next two years whether you like it or not.

It is difficult to write projects, obtain funding, order equipment, install/debug and launch much of anything in less than two years from the time you make your commitment. Small changes or small businesses can react faster, but in general two years is a good rule of thumb. Another issue which must be considered is one that is more subjective but one which you must understand. Any change comes with the need for a paradigm shift. Mindset changes take time and cultural changes take longer. So even if you physically pull off a change in production technology or process in a short period of time, you must take into account the time to change the plants human resources unwillingness to change. Change disrupts your team's comfort level. Therefore you must address this like any engineering issue and be prepared to spend time moving the resistance to change. It has to be an integral part of your technology integration roadmap and game plan for the plant.

One concept that plant teams should engrain into their mindset is an understanding that all plans are made to be broken. So you can't put on blinders. Just understand your plan and the critical path in your plan. If a change is not on the critical path, or it is out more than 2 years, it usually can be adjusted. Having all the answers and a sold plan are not, in reality, attainable. What is important is getting to the point were the team drives the plants' future.

If you have ever had the opportunity to step away from the plant operating level for a period of time and move into the front office, it will surprise you how fast you will loose the pulse and feel of the operation. You loose the feel for what can be accomplished in a plant and how the operating people think. This is critical and must be comprehended so you know what can and cannot be done without major mindset changes. For this reason and this reason only, the plant level operating team must take some responsibility for plant level strategic decisions in future years. Plant teams do not usually realize how much power they have. They are the ones who must carry out the plans and launch new products and technologies. If a plant level team does not buy into a plan, it simply will not happen in any sort of method which you would define as a quality event.

The Technology Roadmap

Once you defined your business, benchmark your competition, understand the gamesmanship required to get things done, identify the paradigms that hinder progress, know your customer and finally identify the technologies which you want to pursue, you're ready to put together a technology roadmap. Once you understand how far you can stretch your current level of technology, then you can outline the next steps through the technology roadmap. A roadmap is just what it says: a project time plan that summarizes the potential benefits for your plant. For example:

Technology	Timing	Potential Improvement
A. Revised Process	Jan XXXX	Reduced Labor cost
B. New Machine	June XXXX	Cycle Time Reduction
C. Material Change	Feb XXXX	Reduced Cost/Improved Performance
D. Integrate	July XXXX	Cost Save through Vertical Integration
E. Expand Plant	Three Years	Projected Volume Increases Due to Productivity

Thick, detailed extensive business plans seem to be the norm that have been put together by companies for corporate review or those that are developed by specialists for start up companies looking for venture capital. This degree of sophistication is not necessary for a plant. What you need in manufacturing is a clear-cut one-page plan with just enough definition to communicate the plants' strategy to all your employees, peers and other members of the management. It should include all the elements of what it takes to maintain a fast follower of technology position. You should of course have back up analysis in sufficient detail that shows that the plan makes financial sense for the plant and the company.

EP's Story Part #5—Be a Fast Follower of Technology

Dennis again called his staff together to discuss next steps. He opened the discussion saying, "we have come to the conclusion from our benchmarking studies and the teams visit to the technology shows that the next generation of toys will have flexible circuit boards molded into the plastic. The process looks like it will require that our plant to insert flexible circuit boards into our injection molding machines and shoot the plastic around the circuits. So what we need to do is put together a plan to get there in the next three years. Since we know how to get this technology and equipment from data obtained from DG's benchmarking trips, I think the approach we should take is to meet with the marketing and product engineering people to let them know we are aware of this evolution and are capable and understand what it will take to move in with this new technology in a very short time frame."

"That is a good idea," said Barb. "In that way we will be proactive. We will most likely surprise them with our aggressiveness and that should give them the warm feeling that we want to be a player. It is not normal that plant people introduce new concepts to marketing and engineering."

DG took over the discussion at that point saying, "we will start discussion on design for manufacture so that we can get down to ordering equipment in the final 24 months prior to production. Establishing some preliminary design guidelines will give us the ability to calculate how much new equipment to add to our plant base and what we can use from our existing pool."

Mary questioned DG on his aggressiveness asking him how he could be so confident when she thought all these new processes had to be invented.

DG responded; "we are not inventing the technology but being a fast follower. If you remember, EP manufacturing started a little skunk works activity to develop a knowledge base for this technology and identify the issues and roadblocks to launching the concept and making that launch a quality event. And second, our benchmarking trip identified who has the technology and I think we will be able to sign a technology sharing agreement with a company that is not in the toy business."

"Now I understand what you mean by being a fast follower," said Mary. 'This is getting exciting. I was thinking I would have to come up with a huge research and development spending account for which I had no concept how we would justify the expenditures."

Barb said, "and what is more, this skunk works can also be used to build the prototypes for marketing. Being the logistics manager I always worry about how we are going to build prototypes especially with some new technology involved. So now we have a plan and where with all to pull it off."

At that point in the discussion Dennis looked at Mary and directed her to put together a one page business plan and technology roadmap that could be reviewed with the plant personal.

Mary then asked Dennis what he had in mind. "I would suggest highlighting that fact that EP is not inventing the technology, but having benchmarked other industries, can now be a fast follower. I would suggest that we even have an opportunity for a technology agreement. EP doesn't compete with the companies that develop the concepts so agreements are possible. Technology sharing agreements will keep our development costs down, and best of all, it will keeps us in the game. "I think that type if comment should be in the opening statement so our people and our upper management team understand how we will approach the future," said Dennis. "Then, I think you should have small technology roadmap with a tentative time which you can get from DG. It should look something like this." Dennis put the following items on conference room blackboard:

Milestone	Timing	Comments
Sell Concept	March to July	Dennis and Ad Hoc Team
Re-design for Manufacture	July to December	Joint Engineering Team
Capacity Study	November	DG's Team
Order new Facilities	December	Dennis to Sell
Build Prototypes	September	Barb to co-ordinate
Test Prototypes	Sept to January	Customer
Get Okay to Proceed	February	Parent Company
Install New Facilities	Feb plus One-Year	DG's Team
Production Start	24 Months	Assumes No Job Stoppers

Barb looked at the timing plan and commented on the item which indicated that the equipment would have to be ordered in December before the plant got the go ahead to proceed.

Dennis responded. "We want to get the jump on our competition and I don't want to be waiting around for equipment to be built. As you know, once equipment suppliers have orders, the word will leak out on what we are doing. So what I will need Mary to do, since she is the plant controller, is write a mini project so we can ask for long lead funding. That project should include cancellation costs that we will have to absorb if we don't get the go ahead or the testing does not come out as expected."

"Do you think we can get that signed?" asked Mary.

Dennis said, "we will if we do a good job at presenting our concepts for the long term viability of the plant. If we don't? Well at least we weren't siting around waiting for the industrial world to pass us by."

With that direction, the team went off to start on the roadmap, technology plans and communication plans to sell the concepts.

Key Take Away Thoughts

If you're not a leader or a fast follower, you're not in the game. And if you're not in the game, you will not have a plant or product with a future. Technology is moving at a constant pace. Continuous improvement is the requirement of the day. If you can't address this experience principal, then you haven't done your benchmarking homework. Equipment suppliers aren't technology leaders in processing and they are not the ones to talk to. You need to take what they have and adapt it for your needs and then keep those little nuisances of change in your hip pocket. Keep in mind;

• You must stay at the forefront of technology for your operation.

• You have choices, but the best approach is to be the fastest follower in technology.

• To follow, you have to understand technology when you see it.

• If you don't have it, it is new technology as far as you are concerned.

• Try to maintain your equipment and keep up with technology—the best of all worlds.

• Two years ahead of the competition is as good as it gets.

• Make sure your plant has and continues to maintain a technology roadmap.

• If you are so far behind that you can't run fast enough to be a fast follower or your facilities constrain your abilities, then you must develop a leap frog technology which is one that is way beyond what the industry is doing—obviously this takes risk.

Experience will tell you that you can either drive your plants future or you will be relegated to live with the outside forces which constantly attack your status quo and like Armageddon, you will relegated to wondering when it is going to get you. In the end remember what Peter Drucker said—"in a competitive global area, costly mediocrity goes out of business. Don't solve problems, pursue opportunity." In other words, you better be technology's fastest follower or you're going out of business.

You can't continue to spin off old technology businesses and buy new. Eventually the house collapses. This is why plants must keep re-inventing themselves. Corporations talk about re-inventing themselves but it is becoming rare that they walk the talk and spend huge sums of money to maintain research and development operations. Thus, it becomes necessary for factory teams to become agile aggressive fast followers of technology.

Experience Principle #6: Communicate, Communicate, Communicate

In the spring of 1998, employees of a General Motors metal stamping plant in Flint, Michigan walked out in a local strike over communication issues that related to a misunderstanding. The issue? General Motors' management agreed to productivity spending levels and did not follow through on that commitment. This local strike spread throughout the company, shutting down operations for months and costing General Motors billions in lost revenue and untold lost wages. At the conclusion of the strike, a key point made by the company and the union was that they needed to set up better lines of communication. They should have told the employees what was being done in the plant relative to the commitments made to improve the technology and age of the equipment in the plant. Many of the salaried employees, as well as the hourly, stated there was more communication during the strike than they ever remembered. It was the first time they knew what was going on within their own plant. Those comments were a major indictment of the company management. The plant management teams were not talking to the employees. That lack of communication not only resulted in lost revenue, but cost the Company market share (which is the hardest thing in any industry to get). Most likely, it also destroyed a lot of careers, both in the company and the union.

Every survey taken over the last 30 years on the subject of what people think is important in the workplace have come back with two items. They are always in the top five and usually the top two needs of employees:

1. Employees "want in" on what is going on—or stated in the vernacular of my experience principles, employees want to know the game plan and the business strategy for the plant.

2. Employees want to know that what they are doing is appreciated—or again stated in the vernacular of this book, you need to scratch the employees "itch"—tell them when they are doing a great job but also tell them when there are problems.

Wages, security, etc have always been down the list on what is important in the workplace. This is hard to believe but has been consistent for all industries and previous phases of "Industrialution". General Motors proved the surveys are right. In a plant environment, communication is critical and the GM strike is about the best example of why this experience principle is so important. History on communication issues constantly repeats itself and I have seen the results in every plant I worked in during my 35 years in manufacturing—if you don't communicate the game plan, you eventually lose control of your operation.

How You Communicate in a Plant Environment

Effective plant level communication requires several approaches. Articles in plant newspapers, updates at routine plant meetings, annual state of the plant meetings and walking the floor soliciting one on one discussion are the key approaches. You need to get the issues and concerns out in the open.

There are a number of different routines that a plant can follow to get the short-term programs and plan information across and I have tried them all. What seems to work best is a combination of all of the following:

*   Daily Meetings with the plant's line supervisors to review the day's requirements for raw materials, purchased parts, productivity requirements, logistics issues, etc.

*   Weekly meetings with the management team to review performance to budget

*   Individual department meetings

In order to communicate the long term issues and concerns, I found "State of the Plant" meetings to be very effective. The presentations should be short (20-30 minutes) and consist of easy to understand charts and graphs with key points highlighted on some type of overhead or slide presentation. The accent on simple is not to indicated that educational level of your employee or management team is limited, but an attempt to get the point across in manner in which employees will remember the message. Advertisers have found that to get products across to the general public, commercials must be short, to the point, and repeated often. So you need to first tell your plant team the game plan, come back in a few months and give them the same information, and follow that up with a presentation at a later date after the people had time to absorb what has been said. There is a theory called the theory of "8's". Simply stated, you must tell people the same thing 8 times before they get the message. Maybe you didn't give them the message eight times, but there is word of mouth and employees discussing aspects of the plans so that by the time is sinks in they may have heard it more than you realize. In a plant environment, this is critical. Everyone must be marching to the same message if you expect to succeed. It is not important you become a marketing expert, but it's important that you understand that the first part of selling the plants future is getting "buy in" from the plant employees. Sales start with your own employees. If you can't sell them, you will not sell your mission and products to the system/bureaucracy.

Routine meetings are needed for day to day issues. State of the plant meetings start the ball rolling on informing to employees that relate to long term issues. However, experienced plant managers have found that the real key to keeping employees up to speed and meeting those two critical elements of employee wants (noted on the previous page) is an interpersonal sales pitch with the operating people. In my years of experience, the most successful plants use an approach similar to a door to door salesman where management teams walk the floor and discuss the game plans, business strategy and whatever customer "itch" is currently causing customer concerns. My experience observing different plant managers has constantly proven to me that this is the most effective way to get information down to the plant floor. Plant teams must be seen and heard on a personnel basis. One on one goes a long way. It is no different than a politician getting out in the streets and plant gates to get his/her message across. You have to do the same thing. It is said that word of mouth is the best advertising. For each person you talk to, statistical studies have shown that the person to whom you talk will repeat what they have heard to five other people. So, members of the plant operating team don't have to have a dialogue with every employee.

There are little games that highlight how important communication can be and how the interpretation may be different than the outcome you expect. These are classic team building exercises. But if you haven't heard about them, here is how they work. Have some of your employees sit on the floor, back to back, and give each one a set of building blocks. Tell them they are going to build together a structure based on your instructions. Than, verbally give them step by step instructions on what to build. As each one assembles their respective structure, continue to give instructions until enough process steps have been communicated to form a structure. When each is done, compare the structures. It will surprise you how both have built a completely different looking structure. That is what will happen to your plant's processes and plans if you don't religiously communicate. You will have one plan in your mind, and the implementers will put in something completely different. If you haven't done this little test, it is worth it if for only to get you to understand how important the above experience principal is and why the theory of 8's evolved.

Addressing Change

The biggest driver for communication in a plant comes when some fundamental structural changes in the plant's business, product, and/or technologies are planned. Change that results in the way you run the plant, organize the teams, etc. upsets people's paradigms. I once had an employee who operated the same machine for over ten years, knew it inside and out, and perceived it as his machine. His peers claimed he talked to the machine like it was a pet. His wife told their friends that the machine was all he talked about at the evening super table—it had become his whole life. When the day came to tell him that technology had moved forward and his machine no longer fit into the plant's future, you can only guess how traumatic a moment that must have been for him. Of course, no one wanted to tell him. Had our plant management team started him, and the rest of the human resources in the plant down a path informing them of changes that would occur in the plant, it would not have been so dramatic.

There is a cycle of change that occurs in every operation and it takes a transition curve in a person's mind to accept these changes. People must get a prepared long ahead of time if you expect them to be part of the team helping the transition to occur smoothly. As shown in Figure 1. the emphasis on constant communication is the only way you get through the transition as change affects everyone's comfort level.

The Transition Curve...Cycle of Change

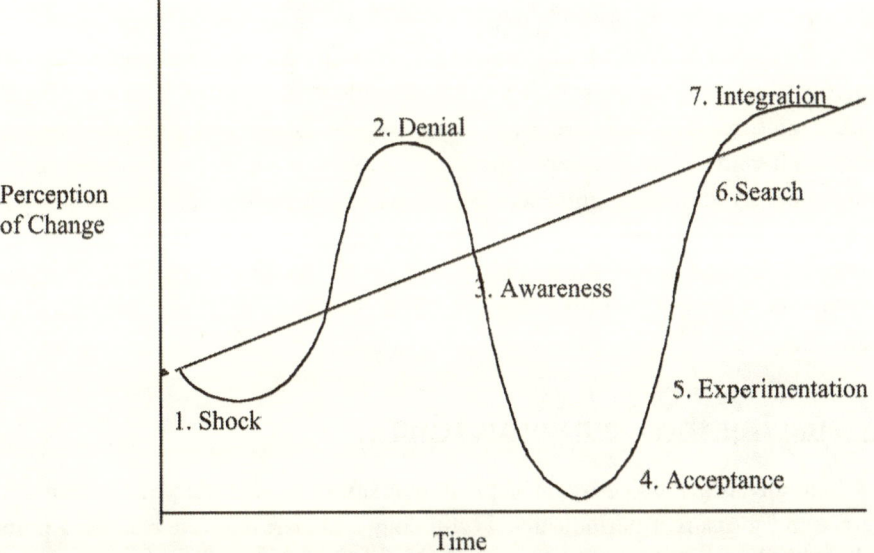

Figure 1.

At first, there is <u>shock</u> or surprise. In extreme cases, there could be panic like in the individual we noted who had grown to see his machine as an individual. This is an employee's perceived mismatch between expectations and reality. Second is <u>denial</u> of the change. The change is not necessary and of course management is just rattling their cage for some other reason. At this point, communication becomes very important as you now must progress through the theory of 8's and constantly take time to communicate this change in all the forms I noted earlier. The third phase becomes <u>awareness</u>. A point occurs when something clicks in the mind of each employee and they will accept the need for change. What causes this awareness to click usually does not have anything to do with the last communication action you took. The employee could be reading about some related item in another company or in the newspaper or hear something on the floor (which might be the seventh, eighth or ninth time he heard it) and all of a sudden it will all come together. It will click in their mind because it has been rolling around in an area of discomfort in the individual's sub-conscience. Some unrelated comment will bring it into focus. At this point, the employee now has awareness and this leads to the fourth phase—<u>acceptance</u>.

Acceptance is letting go of all those past discomforts and paradigms that the plant employees go through during the denial and shock phases. You must pass through this phase to get to the fifth phase called <u>experimentation</u>. This is the place you want your workforce to get to——looking for new approaches to running the plant which will lead to constructive feedback from all the employees on what works and what doesn't. If you haven't allowed sufficient time for the culture to go through each phase, your change will be fought and it can turn ugly in many different ways. The experimentation moves to the sixth phase where the employees <u>search</u> for an understanding of what success will look like when you get there. New procedures will be created, organizations adjusted, and a new operating culture established. The seventh and last phase is <u>full integration,</u> where new skills and mindsets have been developed into a cohesive working environment.

<u>Managing the Communication</u>

Like any other objective in a plant, you must have a communication system—and measure it periodically. Technology and learning have reached a point where "Industrialution" has become a fact of life. Change will be become a constant for all industrial operations and this constant cycle of change means business as un-usual. "Business as Un-Usual" is a phase coined by Dr. Price Praitchett and Dr. Ron Pound. Managing has become a way of life in manufacturing due to restructuring, re-engineering, acquiring, merging, belt-tightening and downsizing. These are all terms that are becoming familiar to anyone working in today's industrial environment. Dr.'s Praitachett and Pound gave us a list of ideas and approaches one can use when walking the floor communicating the game plan and during state of the plant meetings. The ideas these writers identified are noted below. Each one of Dr. Praitchett and Pound's ideas is followed by my interpretation.

- Be a change agent—manage the process

- Don' give away your power, however—you do not want to become tentative

- Keep a positive attitude—be upbeat and positive as you talk to the troops

- Give your team clear-cut marching orders—or as a member of a team, demand them

- Focus on short-range objectives—keep in mind you're trying to keep ahead of the bureaucracy

- Establish priorities—this should have been done as noted in the first chapter

- Nail down each person's job—people need clear cut individual objectives

- Promise change—sell it like everyone knows this is a way of life

- Get resistance to change out in the open—you need to identify the itch

- Raise the bar—you must create stretch objectives if you want to succeed

- Motivate to the hilt—put an energy source into your team

- Encourage risk-taking and initiative—you want access to the brain power of the people

- Don't try to cover all the bases yourself—every team member should have an assignment

- Create a supportive work environment—employees should not feel threatened

- Ride close herd on the transition—success is in the details

- Rebuild morale—it is imperative if to keep the transition curve on track

- Provide additional job know-how—training never ends; it is forever

- Pass out "psychological paychecks"—attaboys go a long way

- Beef up communication efforts—your effort will vary during the stages of change

- Look for bad news—invite it, since you need to know what you are up against

- Protect quality and service—you have to stay in business during alterations

- Re-recruit good people—talented people should be treated like new recruits

- Take care of the "me" issues in a hurry—you need team members to succeed

- Play the role of therapist—you have to handle the emotion changes as well

- Reduce the level of job stress—minimizing surprise with constant communication

- Support higher management—you may not know all the details

- Be a leader—this you have to earn. Don't manage; lead

All of these approaches are aimed at getting the troops through the cycle of change. Life isn't easy today in most industrial operations. It is hard work but if every employee becomes pro-active on the future of the operation and does their best to perform whatever roll they are asked to do, using these ideas will dramatically reduce the personnel stress that occurs when business is not as usual. Most important, employees will be "in" on what is coming in the future and feel appreciated.

EP's Story Part #6—Communicate

The EP Manufacturing operating team realized that couldn't go much further without communicating the game plan. The situation at EP Manufacturing which the team needed to get out to the employees was two fold: EP needed to fix a customer problem that could put them out of business in the short term if it did not get fixed. Second, the plant had to aggressively pursue new technology or it would go out of business in the long term. These issues would affect everyone, as it would change the skill mix in the plant and the product content. Also, the plant may need to add an addition to incorporate this new technology.

Worried about these issues, Dennis stopped in DG's office to discuss his concern about how fast the team was moving and the fact that no one, outside of a few key people, knew the plan.

DG said to Dennis, "when you start thinking about everything we have to do this sounds like a lot for one plant."

"Well, it isn't," said Dennis. "Based on my experience, this is typical of what is going on today in most industries. I can best describe life in a plant as do it now—and do it all with less people while you completely disrupt the comfort level of your workforce. And if we are going to be successful, we will have to get every single person in EP manufacturing up to speed and understand the need to react."

"So, how do we communicate the plans and get buy in?" asked DG.

"Let's get Bill in here from human resources so we don't go over this twice. He is the one who will have to take the lead on our communication strategy," Dennis said. "Call Bill and ask him to come to your office."

When Bill arrived, Dennis and DG updated him on the previous discussion. Having just come from a series of seminars on communication, Bill had a lot of ideas and was anxious to try them.

"We should start with a state of plant meeting," Bill suggested. "Let's shut down production for one hour and get all the employees into one area and make a 15-20 minute slide presentation on the state of business. We don't want to go beyond 20 minutes or we will loose our audience. It should include financial figures and quality issues such as notes on one customer concern (itch) and how we tend to handle the problem. The second phase of the presentation should include DG's team results from the benchmarking trips. Dennis, you should then take the podium and tell the plant team what conclusion you drew from the benchmarking trips and what changes the plant has to make in the future to stay in business. Introduce the alterations you see happening in the next few years. If all goes according to what I learned on communication theory, our people will walk out and not remember a thing about the details nor will they comprehend what was presented. But that is the only way to get stared."

"So what happens next?" Asked Dennis.

"Immediately the next day, you need to start walking the floor and selling the game plan and at the same time address any current issues. Like a politician, you have to carry your message to the people. Except in your case, you don't have to kiss babies."

DG found that comment hysterical—Dennis only smiled.

Bill continued. "Each mourning, before the daily grind and meetings start, as EP's plant mange Dennis, it is critical that you spend a half hour on the floor just talking to people."

"What do I talk about and specifically to who," said Dennis.

"You don't have to go to anyone specifically, just approach random individuals. Ask how they are doing and discuss some of the same items discussed in the state of the plant meeting. Using this approach, the workforce will hear about the game plan, current customer itches and strategies for a second time. However, now you can be more detailed and tell them how it may affect them personally. You should also make sure to hit on the customer issues and new initiatives as part of the general update. Most importantly, don't leave until you ask for input from the employee. Unfortunately for you, this same daily walk-around will be required for an afternoon and night shift. To be seen in casual conversation and letting people in on the know is critical. They will ask questions which helps to alleviate any perceptions of management keeping plans secret—in this way they become part of the team. It is critical you download as much detail as they can absorb."

"How long do I have to make the daily walk-around?" Asked Dennis.

"In my opinion," said Bill, "as long as you are plant manager. It is a fact of life that you have to communicate with you employees continuously. You need to give them the feeling they are "in the know" on what is going on in the plant and you're considering their ideas. That can only be accomplished if they hear it from you in a one on one situation."

"Wonderful," said DG. "That means I will get some free time when the plant manager won't schedule one of these drop in my office ad hoc meetings."

"Be careful," said Dennis. "Don't forget who gives you your performance review and merit raises."

"Let's move on. What else?"

"I have a thought," said DG. "We can have our skunk works supervisor write an article for the plant newspaper on the new technology and what they are doing. The month after that, I can write an article on the plant expansion that we are tying to the new technology. At the same time, Vito can update the people on the customer issues."

"Now you have the idea," said Bill. These follow up actions will support the original state of the plant presentation and, in time, the message will start to come through."

"This sounds good to me," said Dennis. "But don't forget, we still have our weekly operating meetings. These meetings usually concentrate on the issues at hand and I think we should leave it that way. One little "itch" that Vito is trying scratch is a near term problem and this should be on the hit parade at every weekly meeting until it is resolved."

Bill ended the dialogue saying, "this is great stuff. Word will eventually get around that EP's management is being open and honest and while the plant floor people are doing their day to day work, which gets boring, they will feel part of the future and believe that their opinions count. And if we are smart, what they have to say will be taken into consideration."

"I am starting to see that the biggest benefit will come from walking the floor and getting down to the root cause of all the issues with no one in between to filter out critical information," said Dennis. "When I had a staff job, a few years back, it is amazing how one can loose the feel for the pulse of a manufacturing operation and the critical issues when you not on the floor regularly."

"That's the key," said Bill. "But I want to caution you that the whole process doesn't take weeks or months, but years. Overlaying this on the two year planning cycle I heard the both of you talk about," emphasized Bill, "requires that communication must go on concurrently if we as a plant team are to be successful. By the way, in my communication seminar we learned about the cycle of change. I don't want to go *through that here, but it is a concept I think we need to take all the salary people through so they understand how change affects the workforce."*

"Yes I think I just read something on that," said Dennis. "I don't remember all the details but I remember enough that my thought at the time was we had better prepare our resources for change and the cycle of change is something they need to understand. So schedule a little mini course for the troops–Bill."

EP's management team began to realize that for a good plan to be implemented successfully, all the people concerns and motivational issues that were listed in the summary from "Business as Un-Usual" would have to be addressed. EP's management thought they understood the plan after the benchmarking studies and putting a strategy plan together. But until they get feedback from the operating side, the full scope of what has to be done will not be fully understood. Walking the floor and constant communication is the only way that will happen. Only then can details be addressed such as how you deal with the individual we mentioned earlier who got so close to his machine that he talked to it and discussed its operation at home over the supper table. His machine technology would soon be relegated to a previous round of "Industrialution". But you can't afford to loose him to the last round. You need to bring him into the next level of "Industrialution."

Key Take Away Thoughts

Assuming you have defined your business and launched your new product, plant, technology, or added resources, you are ready for the day to day manufacturing agenda. What is it? What do good operating teams do to assure performance to their objectives and customer wants? There are several things:

- Understand that employees want in on what is going on

- Don't manage—lead

- Be a change agent

- Manage communication just like any other project

- Understand accountability. Make sure everyone knows they are accountable

- Understand the cycle of change; build it into you program management system

In day to day operations, things happen so fast that you must meet daily or weekly and talk through all the issues. The discussion between all attendees is critical to get all opinions and everyone's input. If plant meetings include individuals who constrain communication, then some of the employees have interpersonal skill problems. However, if you are the problem—listen to the people. If your boss is the issue, you should let him know that the meetings will be more open and productive if he or she is not in attendance. People are more open when in a meeting with their peers. If managers or supervisors are in the meetings that rate performance of other individuals who are in the meeting, then the discussion becomes somewhat guarded. In a manufacturing meeting, arguing, disagreements, yelling, pounding on the table, and general venting are very important. You can't do that if supervisors or managers of the peer ground attend. *Harmonious (Zen like) daily plant meetings are a sign that either your team is not open to discussing the issues, or you have a very loose budget*—another one of experiences that are rarely wrong or very far off base.

Once a week, as noted in the discussion above, should be performance rating day. You have to give on the spot performance appraisals in manufacturing as it is a business that can't wait. Once a week is as far as you can let it go before the plants operating team reviews activity, issues, quality, budget, etc. The once per week meeting should go into details on performance to budget, quality status, customer performance appraisals, shipping to schedule, and the hot items. This is equivalent to a coach's half time speech. The troops must be reproached or congratulated. If they produce a good first half, then they must be motivated to continue. If the performance wasn't up to the requirements, than constructive criticism is in order. Unfortunately, in manufacturing you never finish the game it just keeps going and there is always another half—but that is the life you picked.

Communicate, communicate, communicate. It can not be highlighted too often. Understanding communication takes time and must be put it into your planning phases—or you will have situation like General Motors had in 1998 where billions were lost and neither the company nor the employees gained.

Experience Principle #7:
Worship the "4P's"

If you're considering a new manufacturing facility, expanding the current plant or adding a new product/process/technology, operational management should address and understand the following:

- Is this a totally new <u>product</u> for the plant?

- Will they have to develop a new <u>process</u> technology?

- Does this mean a new <u>plant</u>?

- Will the plant have to hire new <u>people</u> not familiar with the processes?

<u>P</u>roduct, <u>P</u>rocess, <u>P</u>lant, and <u>P</u>eople are the "**4Ps**". Inside the four walls of manufacturing they are everything. (Note: in some industries, such as a chemical processing plant, equipment is not contained within the physical walls of a building, but imaginary walls or fence lines that surround the manufacturing area.) Whether you have an existing facility or plan to build a new one, this discussion is still relevant. Make sure you read and understand the "4Ps" before you move forward with any plans for expansion. In fact you should not only understand but worship the "4Ps", as they are your only savior if you plan to make major changes to your operation in size, product, process, people, etc.

The key to the "4Ps" is not knowing what they represent, but making sure you do not change all of them at one time. This principle is critical. If each experience principle discussed in this book related to a hole on a golf course, this one would be the number one handicap hole. The optimum change is one "P". One can usually handled with the normal manufacturing team. Changing two of the "Ps" is possible and can be done as a quality event, but it will require you to designate some individuals as part of a launch team and temporarily absolve them of their normal duties. Changing three of the "Ps" will not be a quality event and if you dare to change four, you better plan for financial chaos. When you change four, this is truly a revolutionary change, not an evolutionary change.

Entrepreneurs historically followed these principles without realizing that is what they were doing. Henry Ford built his first engine in his garage and ran it on his kitchen sink. Hewlett and Packard built their first electronic device in their garage. In both cases, the garage was the plant and the inventors were the people with development experience behind them. They only changed two of the "Ps"—the product and the process. Once these inventions were developed, the inventors went to the next phase—plant and people. Subsequently, the plants evolved and processes changed, but at an evolutionary rate. Not all four of the "Ps" were changed at the same time.

What Works

I suggest only changing one "P" if possible, and two at the most. However, this is your call. The process of making the decision of how many of the "4Ps" to change comes under the category of risk-taking. Leadership demands risk-taking. Risk-taking creates discomfort with whoever will profit or lose by the risk. How far you can go and how many "P's" you want to change depends on, as we discussed in the business element, the game you must play. The smaller and more nimble your plant, the greater your flexibility at taking risk. If your plant is part of a bureaucracy where there are complex union contracts, environmental issues, etc associated with making changes, then the system is much more adverse to risk-taking. Another item to consider is how close you are to your customer base. For a plant that is shipping just in time with low inventory and a customer that is selling all the product produced, the risk becomes major if more than one "P" is changed. If the opposite is true and you can afford some flexibility in delivery, more risk can be considered. Whatever you do, remember this principal and practice it religiously.

Small Is Beautiful

You will find, if you benchmark enough, that the best run plants can stay under control if they are small operations, one where you can walk the floor or the plant site and get your hands around the problems, people issues, etc. Small varies by industry. Small may be manufacturing in plants sized in the 10,000 to 100,000 square feet whereas chemical processing plants and steel mills are measured in acres. Only you can define the right size which will be intuitively obvious if you are open and honest with yourself. You must get a feel for the plant that you are running or your portion of the operation and make sure it is not running you. Build a large unwieldy plant, and it will destroy you like a cancer.

The "4Ps" become critical when business exceeds your ability to contain manufacturing in the current facility. You must now decide to expand or build a new greenfield site. Issues can be handled if you stay within the "4P" guidelines and keep it small. A good catch phrase to remember in the world of manufacturing is that **"small is beautiful"**. When building or adding to an existing facility, the plant should still remain small—where small is defined as manageable. A thousand people in 100,000 square feet of manufacturing space may not be small, whereas 200 people working in a one million square foot facility could be considered small. Small means manageable—the ability to get your arms around the business. Small will vary by industry and the amount of automation. There is no formula for the definition of small. However, you will know it is not small if the plant tends to run you vis-a-vis you running the plant. The feeling is obvious when the system is running the place and not the management team (the system being all those unwritten rules, procedures, mindsets, and paradigms that people believe are gospel).

If this is the case, there are solutions. If you are stuck with an unmanageable operation, re-structuring the building does not necessarily have to be costly. The easiest is to break the plant up into mini-plants. This can be done by taking areas of the plant and organizing them into operating teams where the team leader is in fact a mini plant manager of that area. Everyone working with that part of the operation reports to that mini plant manager. If walls can be erected between the areas, that is even better. Once that has occurred, then each of these mini plant mangers or the area management teams establish the game plan for their individual areas utilizing the experience principals.

What Are Your "4P" Options

A manufacturing operation comes in many different forms in a variety of industries. Regardless of the industry, there are a common set of disciplines which should be addressed when building a new greenfield manufacturing site or adding new manufacturing capacity to an existing site.

If you have a current manufacturing operation and new capacity is needed, but you are out of floor space or land at the current location, you have four options:

- Build a satellite facility

- Do nothing

- Build a new self contained manufacturing facility

- Expand the current facility

The decision to build a new self contained operation will be based on the inability to expand the current plant or you have developed a substantial customer base in a different country or area in the country in which you currently manufacture. A satellite facility is a new plant, which usually is somewhat smaller than the parent plant and can be run by the parent plants management team in a way that is similar to adding a new department in the current facility. Usually the driver for this approach is getting the manufacturing operations closer to the customer minimizing transportation costs. The benefit to a satellite facility is one plant manager, one controller's office, one quality office, etc. This reduces fixed costs and overhead costs that come with a separated management team. Obviously this option is very cost effective due to reduced staffing as long as it is small enough to be handled in a remote control fashion.

If and when the business needs to grow for the satellite, there will come a time when the parent plant's management team starts to loose it's "hands on feel" for the satellite and the ability to effectively run the satellite. At that point, a separate management team can be added and this can usually be done without missing a beat in the day to day operations. The other benefit to starting off with a satellite facility is the ability to train personnel at the parent plant. Once trained, they can be moved to the satellite. Common equipment can be de-bugged at the parent plant with the experienced operating team and then moved to the satellite. This approach accelerates the training evolution and is a good method to bring a new plant up to speed faster and more efficiently using the experience base in the core facility. Using the satellite approach to expand your business means your core plant stays small and your new plant stays small and you can use the resources of the core plant for the new maintaining keeping some of the "4Ps" in check. There are no good rules of thumb or ground rules for deciding when a plant can no longer be controlled as a satellite. With communication links today, and the ability to transfer data, inventory, E-Mail, etc. electronically running a satellite facility is becoming a common and viable option for most operations.

You also have the option to do nothing. This is an option sometimes forgotten. Sales are always cyclic and some businesses have extremely high peaks and extremely low valleys. This is called amplitude in a sine curve and is derived from periods of under-capacity to periods of over-capacity. It is more cost effective to level your volume spikes and still fill your customers needs. In some cases you just may want to turn down business for those peak periods which usually do not last too long in the life of a plant. Trying to meet those peaks can be very disruptive to the workforce and you can get yourself into a hiring and laying off mode. It also requires a lot of assets to handle the peak operating patterns which become non-peak very fast and you have tremendous carrying costs to keep the underutilized facilities in a standby mode waiting for the next order or upturn in the business cycle. Boeing Aircraft was in this mode in the 60's. When they received a major order or designed a new aircraft, Boeing hired thousands of engineers. When the project was completed, they were laid off. In those days, it was known around the engineering schools that if you wanted to be an engineer and work your way up to driving a taxi, go to Seattle. Of course, Boeing finally realized how disruptive that was and eventually stabilized the work force at least to a level that stopped the jokes. So, a decision not to expand capacity is an option and should always be the first option.

Highly automated plants tend to be very inflexible to change. Management teams get excited over automated plants but soon find they create a lot of bottlenecks which can not be easily resolved due to the excessive integration of automation. It creates a lack of flexibility to make changes. All these issues are examples of the complexity of change which are magnified dramatically each time you add a change to one of the "4Ps".

EP's Story Part #7—Addressing the "4Ps"

Based on DG's capacity calculations, EP Manufacturing needed a building addition to add this new technology called insert molding of electronic circuit boards. The technology required placing the flexible circuit boards into the plastic injection molding machines and squirting the plastic resin into the molds encapsulating the circuit boards. In the past, EP molded the plastic parts separately and made the circuit boards in a traditional process and assembled the two prior to shipment.

DG decided he needed to get his key process engineers together to go through the process and put together a plan to get this new technology into the plant, handle all the issues and keep production going on day to day business.

DG opened the dialogue saying, "EP's plant is small and manageable. By definition we want to keep it that way as we incorporate this new technology. The management team knows everyone and can get their hands around the day to day operating issues. We, or at least I, don't want to loose that feeling of control. So, do we add on to the current plant, go with a satellite facility, or build a new facility and let some other management team set it up and run it?"

"I don't understand," said Norm who was DG's process engineer. "If you want to keep control of the plant, how do you do that if you build a new standalone facility someplace else."

"Exactly the problem," said DG. "If we elect to build a new plant, then it means a new management team. Someone else will incorporate the new technology and our little facility will slowly fade away."

"I don't like that idea,' said Norm.

"Nor do I," added George from industrial engineering.

"However, we have to do what is best for the company," said DG. "If a new facility is proposed, it could be small but it will mean new people, new plant, a new process, and a new product. This does not appear to be the smart play. We will end up changing all of the "4Ps". A satellite facility, however, could be near our customer's plant. It is feasible and we could reduce end item inventories; EP could ship production hourly or less at a just in time rate. It would require a new process, new people, new product, but not necessary be considered a new plant. The new equipment could be brought into our current facility where the people and plant were the same and just the product changed. The process and product issues could be debugged and the satellite employees trained before they went into the new plant. In that way, EP would have to launch a new plant but only after the product, process, and people were up to speed. Using this approach, EP can get started by tackling only two of the four "Ps"…process and product. Later, we could take on the third "P" called people—except they would be trained in the current facility. When all was ready, the entire operation would be moved to the new satellite facility and once again only one of the "Ps", plant, would be changing. In this way, EP could split up the "4Ps". Since it would be a satellite, the office staff and the engineering department would be the same. We would not be changing that portion of the people resources."

"*That sounds like a reasonable plan and would reduce shipping costs and inventory,*" *noted Harry EP's production supervisor.* "*But what about the final concept—keep it all in house in the current facility? I would end up with all this excess capacity when our current machines are shut down, which seems like a waste of investment money to me.*"

"*Let's pursue your thought,*" *said DG.* "*To keep the product in house, EP would have to expand and get some new equipment to handle the transition. That would only require changing two of the "4Ps", product and process. Additionally, the new process would be replacing the old one so in the end the plant would still be small and manageable even though it would somewhat physically bigger (floor space would have to be added). For the satellite scenario, all the "Ps" eventually would change but be done in an orderly phased approach. This would take much more time and most likely, in the real world, add at minimum one year onto the launch phase of the project.*"

"*Yeah, and since time is the key to the game*", *said George,* "*we have to remember that we need to stay ahead of the bureaucrats to survive the game of manufacturing.*"

"*Sounds like the best plan is to go with a plant expansion and keep everything in EP's current facility,*" *said DG.* "*The key item in this plan is that EP already has resources trained in the complementary technologies so this new technology would only be an incremental step in EP's training plan. Therefore, unless the customer demands a facility nearby, then the overall best plan for EP is to expand their current plant with hopes of follow-on business to fill up the area which will eventually be vacated when the new processes are in production. Since I think we all agree, let's go with this plan.*"

Key Take Away Thoughts

Listed below are some of the experiences I believe are critical that you follow:

- Never change all "4Ps"

- Keep a plant small—small means manageable

- Understand the key decision items can change your decision matrix as to what country to build a plant—unions, environmental, transportation, tax structure, material availability, tax structure and credits

- Remember, doing nothing is an option

Throughout this book, I will continue to emphasis the importance of the sequence which you must approach the experience principals. How would you decide your next move if you did not develop a strategy during the business element? This sounds obvious, but my experience constantly shows it doesn't always happen. Operational decisions are like playing chess. If you do not have your next sequence of moves in mind when you make an operational move, your plant will eventually put itself into checkmate.

Experience Principle #8: The Buck Stops at the Bottom...Manufacturing

Marketing creates brands, logos, sales strategies and product distribution channels. Sales sell the product. Finance tracts budgets, revenues and profits. Business planning develops strategies and long term plans on a company wide basis. Design and product engineering develop the product and draw up the designs on a CAD system. However, when all these functions complete their job and the planning is complete, have they added value or created a product? The answer is no—there are plans, marketing strategies, sales and financial projections, mission statements, objectives and designs. But there are no physical shippable products. It all gets dropped into the laps of the plant people with the objective to make it happen no matter what the quality level of the information and design. The buck falls to and stops in manufacturing. And as I have found more often than not, the plans and drawings usually lack detail, timing needs and come with politically correct estimates of investment and volume projections vis-a-vis real world projections. But this is the world of manufacturing and you must produce a quality saleable product no matter how poor a job was done by the other activities. Manufacturing gets the buck and can't pass it on.

The Volume and Design Buck

Volume projections are in the job definition of sales and marketing. By nature, however, they will always be optimistic. Can you picture a sales manager sitting in front of his senior company managers projecting flat sales with a new product or something less exciting? It just doesn't happen. However, it may be a year or two later before the accuracy of the sales projections are realized. Manufacturing, on the other hand, must commit to purchase facilities ahead of time to meet marketing's volume projections. That is why my experience has show that the more experienced plant management teams purchase the quantity of facilities based on historic volume estimates. Manufacturing is held accountable for the depreciation of under utilized equipment when projections do not materialize. Of course, if the marketing volume projects turn out to be right, then the plant team has to be held accountable if they can make sufficient quantities of the product. But that is the way it is in manufacturing.

If the design needs to be adjusted at the 11th hour and it affects timing or developed slips versus the marketing plan, the miscues always fall to manufacturing. Plants must deliver a quality product designed for manufacture that fits the customer's wants and needs. Delivery must be on time and consistent with a customers order no matter what organization in the planning through design phase misses projections, timing, design changes, etc. And manufacturing must deliver in a way that is perceived as a quality event. I have never seen a product that didn't require product redesigns and volume adjustments after the tooling was completed and facilities installed.

Not to many years ago I was involved in a program that was the ultimate example of what can happen. A newly designed product was so late that the product designers couldn't work out the design details and get prints released for the project before tool construction had to start. As a result, the designers moved forward to meet their timing deadline. A blueprint was released with no lines, no drawing and no information on it except a little notation. The notation indicated the name of the part and a signature next to an official stamp which said "ok to tool and produce". Manufacturing was given a blank sheet of paper with a signature. It sounds like I prefabricated this but it is a true story—and it happens a lot. Design passed the buck. And, as usually happens, the buck stopped at manufacturing's door since there was no one left to pass it to. With the clock running, my team had to do something to get the buck moving. What we did was review the air cleaner designs we had been manufacturing. Based on the space available in the vehicle and current designs, we made a gut call on what the air cleaner should look like. But would it perform? Who knew? However, we got started. Our prototype shop built a quick working prototype for testing and design evaluation. Testing on the prototype was conducted simultaneously with tool construction. Following the tests, we had to make major changes to the tools. Of course it required a major tear-up to adjust for all these changes. At the end, however, we got the job done and made the production dates. Examples like this are why I believe that the buck stops in manufacturing and you never know what the buck will look like—or least it has never failed in my thirty-five years in manufacturing.

The Expansion Buck

Assuming you make the decision to build a new facility or purchase some existing building or plant, location is everything. Location, location, location are the first three things to consider. First you must look at the infrastructure of the area or country in which you are planning to build. Infrastructure means support for everything you need: utilities, taxes, political stability, technical support resources, utilities, and transportation. For example; aluminum smelting costs are very sensitive to electric power rates. You would not want an aluminum operation in an area of the country where electricity costs were high. Since the lowest electricity costs are in areas that are fed by hydroelectric plants, your first location considerate should be in an area where there is an ample supply of hydroelectric power. Historically, steel mills were located around the Great Lakes areas in order to get iron ore from the Messobe range in Minnesota by freighter. Today, with the advent of electric furnace technology and mini-mills, that location scenario is no longer a necessary requirement and the driver may be electricity costs instead of access to iron ore.

Buying land for a plant sounds simple, but it is not. There are four considerations that can change your decision on land acquisition from something as minor as to what partial to buy to what country in which to build the plant. The issues that are becoming major considerations and can expect to add over a year into your planning phase include:

- Political Stability of the Local Government
- Tax Structure
- Environmental Issues—wetlands, etc.
- Zoning
- Supply Infrastructure and Shipping

Political stability and tax structures vary dramatically throughout countries and within countries. When communism died, many American and western European companies wanted to build or buy plants in eastern Europe. One company of which I am aware of went property shopping and when they found the location they thought was desirable, they asked who owned the land and whom they should approach to make an offer. In a communist state, the people own all the land and all the businesses. Once communism fell, what would seem to be a simple matter was not. No one knew who owned the land. After a prolonged investigation, which held up the plant project, it was concluded that the company had to go back in time and find out who owned the property prior to communism. Before the company could take control, they contacted the heirs of the individuals who owned the land prior to communism. They assumed the land reverted back to the original owners and/or their heirs. Based on these assumptions, they made offers to purchase the property. The owners accepted, but would not take anything except hard western cash. To close the deal, the company had to collect the property owners, put them on a bus, and drove them to a bank in the largest city that could handle the transaction. Each owner was paid off in cash. This example may seem a little abnormal, but it emphasizes the complex issues that can arise. Purchase of land in today's environment is not simple and can easily add a year onto your whole project. It can be one of the bigger bucks that stops in the laps of a manufacturing team.

There are other examples of issues that emphasize the complexity of new plant decisions. Here are a few more:

- In the most developed countries, and almost everywhere you go to look for a place to build, you will run into areas called "wetlands" or "green laws" which could dramatically change how you plant is built or if it will be built.

- Material prices vary from country to country. In North America, high density polyethylene costs almost half of the prices in Europe. Historically, cast iron in the United States has always been cheaper than aluminum, whereas in Germany, aluminum historically was cheaper than cast iron.

While property acquisition is generally not complicated in developed countries, the impact on your timing plans and effort may be as great. Environmental concerns, local union issues and other community concerns must all be addressed and can be time consuming. Tax credits have driven many decisions as to which states or countries vie for new plants. The ones with the best to offer do not necessarily win, as other things can offset land acquisition savings—such as the local employment or unemployment situation. Tax credits can be very important from a short term financial end but many plant site acquisition teams fail to realize tax benefits eventually end. Back in the 50's and 60's you could build a plant in Brazil, get enough credits to offset your entire manufacturing costs, ship your product, dump it in the ocean and make a profit. The credits totally offset the manufacturing costs.

All the ins and outs come down to the two theories my experience has shown to be true:

1. To effectively sell a product in a country, a company will be driven to manufacture in that country. Governments will drive that need through tariffs, local content laws, etc. (Note: There is, of course, a corollary to the first of these comments——if you don't plan to sell your product in a country, don't build a plant in that country. Your wasting valuable investment dollars.)

2. Chasing low cost labor rates and areas of low or non-union activity is short term thinking. By moving into one of those localities you become the driver for increased labor costs and unions. Sooner or later you will have to address both. You can prove this to yourself if you study the labor rate history of Indonesia and Japan)

As long as you understand and accept them, you can move forward with your strategy to build a plant in any specific country or locality. I would suggest you accept these principals and get on with the business of running your plant as it will save a lot of stress and soul searching.

Issues Requiring Discussion

Unions also vary from country to country and within a country. In Mexico, you will have unions but they are vastly different than the U.S. and will have little affect on your decision matrix, at least to this time. In Great Britain, however, it is just the opposite and may be the make or break decision to build a plant, as has been the case with many companies. Great Britain suffers from to many separate unions required for the same manufacturing location. Having to deal with one union for your facility is difficult enough. But in England, it is normal to have five or six different unions in the same facility—all with different contracts and timing between expiration dates for their contracts. This one issue alone can so disrupt your business and your plant teams ability to handle day to day issues that many manufacturers just will not build new greenfield sites in England. In many European countries, the 36-37 hour work week requirements are forcing plants to leave for other countries. Many pundits tend to think that labor rates drive manufacturers from countries to countries, states to states. However, it is a bigger problem when unions force work rules on your operation that make it all but impossible to handle volume shifts, technology changes, or keep employees on jobs that are no longer needed due to some historic agreement. These bucks or problems tend to fully encompass management's time, making it very hard to do much else.

A lesser but just as important an item relating to plant location is transportation. In North America (Canada and the United States), transportation costs are relatively lower vis-à-vis Western Europe. North American has an infrastructure of highways and rail systems that compete with each other for the transportation dollar. Truckers carry large payloads and the rail system has what are referred to as fast trains. Fast trains don't refer to speed, but rather their ability to be loaded at point A in one area of the country and go to point B at the extreme end of the country non-stop. In Europe, truck payloads are physically smaller and the various countries with their separate rules and regulations make transportation costs higher. The European Community (EC) is starting to change all of that so stay tuned—the decision matrix for Europe will be different in the future. Changes driven by the growing importance of the EC and their drive for unifying all the countries in the EC is a good example of the continuous change driving "Industrialution". Japan's highway congestion is awesome plus land values and fuel costs are high vis-à-vis North America. Japan like Europe, has a miniaturized trucking system that equates to high shipping costs. China just doesn't have roads or vehicles. But once again, times are changing. China is building a interstate/motorway type highway from Hong Kong into the interior. This is the start of a transportation infrastructure that will make the location decision matrix different in the next ten years.

Once you have picked a site, construction can start. You may start construction with a set of parameters and understand your business and customer base. However, in today's changing world, that will not last long. Specifically, do not put your major incoming utilities on the side where you are reserving for future expansion. Also, construct the walls in such a way that those walls are not load bearing. This is a small detail with minor cost at the time of construction but, can be very costly at a future date if these considerations are not addressed early on. You must always be aware that the external and customer environments are in constant change.

There is one last thing to emphasize. "Industrialution" means plants will be forever in a state of change. I have come to believe plant manufacturing technologies, process layouts and material flow will only be stable for two years at the best. You need an understanding of the technology that is evolving and make sure that none of the facilities within your plant become "boat anchors"—a boat anchor is my perception of a piece of equipment which **can not** be moved once installed without shutting the plant down for a periods of time that are unacceptable to the customer. For instance; would you install a blast furnace in a steel making facility at the head of rolling line? Or would you set it in another location? Obviously, if it was at the head of a line you could not take one down without the other and could not add or delete capacity of one without affecting the other. In this case, both the blast furnace and the rolling mill are boat anchors. If production of the blast furnace increased due to productivity improvements or new steel making technology, that increase in productivity could not be utilized if the rolling line productivity did not go up accordingly. Now, if the rolling line was not in line with the furnaces and there were other output opportunities, then the productivity increase could be utilized.

How Do You Address the Buck

What generally happens in a plant environment are that issues, or bucks, come flying in frequently and with such urgency that the intuitive thing to do is move with a quick fix. The issue with the quick fix is that the same problem will occur over and over until the root cause of the problem is identified and a permanent solution implemented. Without fixing the root cause, problem teams always end up working on things that happened in the past. The team never has a chance to get to the phase of doing preventative planning and setting up operational solutions based on predictive if-comes. So you must look into your organization and see if it displays the general signs of a quick fix mentality. These general signs you want to avoid are:

- Assuming everything will go as planned

- Rushing to a solution; letting your anxiety keep you from going through a disciplined root cause analysis

- Failing to identify the real problem, getting preoccupied with getting back into production or solving the problem, and focusing on the incident rather then the system that caused the problem to occur

- Not anticipating the problem, not considering potential crisis issues and deadlines and having appropriate checkpoints to make sure your program is on stream: the occurrence of crisis issues can be minimized by performing a failure mode analysis on a part and/or a process before the product is put into production

- Buck passing confrontation (didn't happen on my shift) rather than collaboration; tagging problems to one bin/shift and assuming that is where the problem lies

What I have found is the best way to handle all issues is to develop a failure mode analysis for everything you do. In other words, you have to start working ahead while the team is still addressing past issues. How can your product fail, how could your process fail, how can your customer disrupt your system with order changes, how can a suppler affect you performance, etc? There are books written on failure mode analysis and I won't go into it deeper in this book. But if you are not familiar with the concept, it is really quite simple. Failure Mode Analysis is a disciplined approach to predict potential problems. The process is one where you write down everything you think could go wrong, rank them in some order of what would be the worst that could happen to what may be minor and identify the probability of solution for that problem. Then you define what has to be done to prevent occurrence of the problem. Once the matrix is developed, you start with the biggest issue and assign a team to come up with a solution ahead of time or a method to prevent the occurrence. In this way, you're working on problems that have some probability of occurring and, if and when they happen, you are way ahead in solution analysis and will not fall into the quick fix tailspin.

What you want to do is manage the process of problem solving and addressing what to do when the buck stops at your door. If it is product or process changes, your team should have an organized plan addressing all elements of the change.

You keep breaking down the elements of the change until you can't go further. This is more difficult than it sounds, but will assure success. There are project software packages on the market that can be used for project planning, which tends to force the team to address all the issues. Success in the manufacturing world lies in the details and the quality of each event in the timing matrix. Most organizations in the decision chain overlook the details and, what is worse, they usually are not aware of the little technical details that are critical. These people are usually a mile wide in knowledge, but only a millimeter deep. There are exceptions, of course.

When the Buck Stops.

The buck usually comes in the form of a major change in the physical plant, a re-organization, a new product or technology, etc. The most effective way to handle the "buck" when it comes flying out of the decision matrix is to put together a launch team consisting of the key operational personnel. A typical team should include individuals with the expertise noted below:

- Manufacturing Engineering
- Process Engineering
- Plant Engineering
- Material Control or Logistics
- Quality/Statistical Knowledge
- Industrial/Plant Layout Ability
- Financial Analysis

As you approach the actual launch, the team should be folded back into the normal operating departments prior to going into production. Normally this time frame will vary depending on your business and you must decide when that occurs.

The first step for a project/problem launch team is to put together a good game plan. By plan, I mean a project timing plan. How long it takes to implement each phase of a new product and process and the interrelationships between each of the process elements. Having done that, you can put together a critical path and define how long it will take to get your new process, plant, technology and/or product into production. Machine "A" will take "X" months to build and it will be installed in a building addition that will take Y months to construct. This is called block timing and will give you an indication when your team should be formed and/or project leader assigned. However, machine "A" may take "X" months to build, but if will also necessitate a period of time to get funding, installation, tryout, etc. These are the details that must be understood. The next thing you do is add specific dates and review the overall timing. A machine or tool that gets completed on time but two months before local frost laws allow shipping, could cause a missed delivery date to a customer's commitment. Success in project planning is in the details.

Establishing a project/problem solving team has another great benefit. Usually manufacturing is at the bottom of the food chain and they must fight for every little detail change that is needed to pull off a successful process or product change. To do that one usually has to go to war with the staffs. And usually in those cases, he who has the biggest arsenal wins—which means you have to overwhelm whatever staff you need to convince to make a change. You have to surface more issues and logical discussion than the other organization can handle.

Expansion usually requires you stay open during alterations so you want a facility and a process that will allow you do to just that. Technologies change, equipment needs change, and as noted earlier in this chapter, if you are keeping abreast of your industry's needs, your plant will change dramatically every few years. Your mindset is to think along the lines of a chess player. Make your moves, develop your project and your time lines, but always keep in the back of your mind a list of all the "if comes" which could affect the physical layout of your plant and how you would respond to any one of those. Obviously you can not address all of them, but you must think out of the box on this one and consider all possible scenarios and future problems. You must identify how they will be addressed. For once you are up and running, you can not make strategic moves very easily. The one thing you hope to avoid, although it is almost impossible, is to add inventory or labor to maintain your ability to keep open during alterations. War room planning ahead of time can offset a lot of this and in the process save a lot of stress on the business. It turns out this is not a complex task, but it is one of those little experiences that I find management teams do not do well. Keep the problem small and in the hands of a few and you can handle change. Make it big and you loose control.

Command and Control

Running your plant means just that—run it. Don't let the plant or your corporate system run the operation. We will get into team concepts and other human resource issues in a later chapter, but to operate a plant in a day to day environment, you must have control at all times and communicate constantly—holding individuals accountable for every element of the operation. This doesn't mean you can only control an operation of process by a direct employee/ boss relationship. There are ways of accessing power and making your peers accountable for items you believe they have to control. No one will necessarily give you the power. Sometimes you just have to take it and run. Management styles continue to float the textbooks. Many support this growing hang loose attitude evolving in society. However, this management style just doesn't work for the discipline needed to run a plant. It is just making it more and more difficult to hold individuals accountable. Since the buck stops in manufacturing, command and control is usually the only management style that will work. Teams require consensus. Consensus requires time. And time is the one commodity you do not have.

Planning for the Buck

To offset all the lack of accountability that occurs outside the manufacturing arena requires planning in very specific detail if the operation is to get products and equipment into production. Planning is one of the forgotten courses in most college curriculums. Until that changes, plant management must recognize this and assume that if you don't have a training program on project planning, you may have to implement an internal intensive course. Up front planning, which includes a list of actions necessary to complete the project and the timing, is a very difficult mindset to establish. Today we live in a society where to many of the young employees have been spoon fed knowledge during their learning years and have not been held accountable to think responsibly. You can see this if you have ever hired a tradesperson for a home project. They will quote you a price, and as soon as the project starts they will invariably come across some obstacle that takes more time than they planned or want to spend and the price will change. In fact, try getting them to write up the specifics before they start. It is very unlikely that they will be able to define all the elements of the job even though they are experienced and have done it for years. It is no different in a plant environment. That is the way management teams need to force the discipline of developing a timing plan. It gets individuals to think responsibly and then be held accountable for the subsequent actions.

You can't live with a lack of planning and execution. You need products tooled up and produced in some time frame at an agreed to cost and at some quality level. You get the "buck" and can't pass it on—your responsibility is to get it through the goal post. This will only happen in a way that is perceived as a quality event if you do the following:

• Have a clear vision of what it is you want to accomplish

• Clarify expectations to all employees/associates/team members

• Assign resources so that the task can be accomplished

• Define responsibility and accountability to individuals

The biggest problem I continue to find in plants is that no one is sure of their tasks or level of responsibility. They are never asked to account for performance to a task. To see if this happens in your organization, attend a problem solving or operating meeting in your plant that your not required to attend. Observe who comes in with the responsibility to report on a problem, who ends up with the assignments and who walks out with a clear understanding they have to answer to that issue. Having done this, I have found, more often than not, no one ends up with specific assignments or responsibilities. Earlier in my career command and control was way of life and no one ever left a meeting not knowing what their assignment was relative to the problem. Today this is not the case. I assume it relates to the casual attitude that pervades society. However, it is an attitude you can not have when the buck sits in your lap.

EP's Story Part #8—Accepting and Addressing the Buck

EP manufacturing benchmarked the industry and knew a major "buck" was heading toward their plant. The buck they saw coming was the new technology that would render EP's facility obsolete. In EP's case, the buck was till coming and could be out at least five years but the management team knew it would come. So, EP had to approach the buck before it could gain so much momentum that they would not be able to stop it. In EP's case, they would have to drive the new technology in order to stay in business.

So, Dennis called his operating team together to talk about this phase of the program and how DG's timing plans would be implemented. Dennis opened the meeting saying, "the approach I want to take, and I would like to get some open dialogue from you, is to convince our parent corporation that this new technology in manufacturing should be an integral part of the future of toy making. We need to convince them that we are in the process of getting the technology. The plan would be to get upper management to accept the proposal and then drive it down to the plant level where we will be waiting and hopefully ahead of any of our competitors."

"I see," said Barb. "The game plan we developed earlier for EP was to recognize the trends in our industry, identify a plan the would give the plant a viable future, and then drive that thought process up the ladder in a slow meticulous way such that senior management believed it was their idea. Then, as the buck gets driven down to the plant floor, EP would already be in a position to react."

"Exactly," said Dennis. "And while we—by the way we means it is your assignment, Barb, along with Bill in human resources—are greasing the skids with our in-house marketing pitch, DG and his team must start to move on the physical plant changes. But that can't wait until the bureaucracy mindset has jelled. So, DG must move forward with a plant expansion needed for the new technology in anticipation of the buck when it comes."

"So, how do you plan to get started DG?" Asked Mary.

DG thought about this for a few minutes and then said, "Dennis you have $100,000 approval authority for new expenditures. But I need to spend $180,000. My project tracking guys do not feel the project will get through the corporate approval process in any time necessary to get a jump on the competition. So instead of writing one project for $180,000, let's split the line detail up in each project and write two. Most likely it will take a little more time but will take far less time to the approval than going through the approval chain so typical for our corporation."

"Why do you need to spend so much?" Asked Mary. "Can't you get away with $100,000, which is within our maximum approval level? I don't like playing games with the system."

"The reason we need to get these projects going is we can't wait for the system to react since my capacity planning department calculated that we will need a building expansion and must get started before winter. The addition will cost more than $100k," said DG. "Once the frost sets in, we could loose four or five months. Also, Dennis and I looked at an expansion versus a satellite facility or new plant. Based on

our concern over the 4P issues, we decided the plant expansion offers the least risk and is cheaper than the alternatives."

"Okay, I understand," said Mary. "But how do we approach the project issue?"

"Let's handle this one like one plant manager I worked for early in my career," said Dennis. "First, DG you write a project with Mary's input, and I will approve it, to build a concrete pad next to the current building. That way we will get the concrete poured before winter and can temporarily use the pad for storage of old equipment and some inventory that does not have to be in the building. When that is completed, or concurrently, write a cost savings project for an overhead crane. We will need a crane for loading molds into the presses if and when that becomes manufacturing space. The cost savings project, however, will be written in such a way to indicate that the crane is needed to handle the storage of molds and other purchase items on the concrete pad. The cost savings will come in the form of reducing the need to purchased added fork lift trucks and the need to hire drivers for those fork lift trucks. If our overall effort to get the approval for this new technology is not acceptable, than the plant could optimize use of the area and save labor associated with forklift truck drivers. So it won't be money sunk without a return."

DG jumped into the discussion saying, "of course, you can't build an overhead crane without having structural steel beams to hold up the crane rails. Once the structural steel is in place, it becomes easy to extend the plant roof over the crane as part of another project already approved to re-do the roof on the main plant. And my construction crew could install some corrugated steel panels on the side of the crane's structural steel I-beams. That could keep the rain out. A third local project for some corrugated steel panel along with a separate project for heaters plus a weekend's effort and we have an enclosed building. Later on, the plant construction crew can tear down the wall between the main plant and this storage area during the time available in between other programs. In this way the plant will ended with a building expansion using petty cash, local projects and overtime for our in-house skill trades."

"I agree," said Dennis. "We won't have to fight the battle with corporate for a building expansion for a business that we are not sure is core or not to the company. But by the time we are done with our in-house marketing pitch, we will be darn sure we are core. We are going to be fast followers of this new technology and let the company know we are in the game to offer this new manufacturing approach before they even know there is a new approach."

"I don't know," said Mary. "Somehow it just doesn't sound right."

"Is it right to sit back and wait until it is to late to change and the company has to write off a major plant, like EP, which will cost more?" said Dennis. "Of course not. Our game plan is not for personal greed, but for the good of the plant and the com-

pany's future. The only thing we are doing is jump starting the system to maintain an advantage. I don't think it is acceptable in today's environment to sit back and let the world go by. If we are to keep EP a viable operation for the company and meet our responsibility to the employees and the community, we need to act or the economic climate in our little town will end up like all those little towns in upstate New York along Mohawk River. They died after the first industrial revolution phased out and when "Industrialution" took hold."

"All right," said Mary. "I'm on board."

Had EP sat back and done nothing, the buck would have come, but when it did, they would not have been in a position to react and in fact would have no concept of what to do. The plant would be closed, people and the community would suffer and the company would have to take a major financial hit and write off the remaining depreciation in the plant. EP knew that their function in life was to add value to a product and as long as they continued to do that in a productive and cost competitive way, they would continue to have a plant with a future.

Key Take Away Thoughts

Earlier, we discussed the "insurance policy" for new plants and processes. This allows one to react to change or bad news. If you decide, after looking at all the alternatives, that a heavy dosage of automation is required for your business, then the next step is to do a "what if scenario" and find out if there is any insurance money you should invest in to protect future changes. Insurance in this case refers to spending additional amounts of money in areas that may not be necessary in the short term, but could affect your livelihood in the future. As an example, there was an automotive engine manufacturing plant who had to install a highly automated machine line. Current product technology required the engine block be made out of cast iron. But there were indications that in the future the cast iron parts would change to aluminum. In general, cast iron is machined dry, whereas aluminum is machined wet. The insurance policy decision was whether or not money should be allocated to install troughs under the machining line before installing the automated machining line. If aluminum blocks never happen, the money would be sunk with no return on the investment. However, if aluminum castings were to become the trend, then the money would be well spent and the same line could be used for machining aluminum blocks just by adding piping for coolant and changing the feeds and speeds of the cutters. Without the trough, the line would have to be completely removed and rebuilt on the spot after the troughs were dug. If this plant waited for the buck to come, the customers would not have waited while alterations were made. Most likely, the cus-tomer would have gone elsewhere and this plant would have lost market share or its business in total and would have to close its doors. The cost of this insurance policy was 10% more for the total investment vis-a-vis what could be a whole new plant or plant expansion if the current production could not be shut down while the changeover occurred. This is not a trivial decision, but it is one that can be made if you did benchmarking and identified trends in the industry. So remember the following:

- Beware of sales projections—you may want protect your facilities by adding your own confidence factor into the projections before you commit resources and investment

- When time is up and you have to get going on plant changes, you may have to grab the design and run even if it is not completed and hope you can adjust later

- Don't let the buck rattle around in your plant; grab it and make someone accountable to address whatever the issue is that comes with buck—command and control are necessary evils in manufacturing

- Stop and plan; plants tend towards the quick fix, since they are always under pressure

- Be creative; use the authority levels you have to address issues and get the ball rolling

- Insurance for the plant is a good thing; insurance being the expenditures for "if come" programs and technologies that will offset investment in the future; however, there is always the risk you will spend the money needlessly

Experience Principle #9: Champion Best Practices

What are best practices? They are a disciplined set of operating procedures that must be done on a routine bases in order to stay focused on the plants mission, which is productive throughput of whatever product the plant manufactures—and those practices must be continuously monitored. If you rear a child and teach him to brush his teeth every night before bedtime, it eventually becomes ingrained and a way of life for the child. It is a best practice in the home. Best practices for plant personnel are no different. They need a set of best practices ingrained into their minds such that it becomes a way of life in the plant—a day to day routine. If plant resources do not follow a set of disciplined practices, then the management team will constantly address annoying miscellaneous issues which occurred in the past and that is not what you want to be doing. You want the plant teams to be working on current production and future opportunities. Management needs to run the plant—the opposite of which is forced into the plant dictating management's time by having to address past problems.

During the course of the rest of this chapter, I will examine some of the best practices I found are critical to a manufacturing operation. These are the day to day items every plant needs to engrain into the mindset of every individual.

Housekeeping Is Productivity

I once worked with a plant manager that noticed whenever his plant's performance to budget was positive, the plant looked extremely clean. He concluded, somewhat wrongly, that if he kept cleaning the plant the performance to budget would always be positive. His logic was flawed, but not altogether off base. When everything is in its place and the equipment is clean, it is a sign that the workforce is disciplined and acceptable to the housekeeping responsibilities inherent in their assignments. And if they accept that responsibility and make sure it happens, you can bet that the performance metrics will follow suit. A machine that may be constantly dirty and is leaking oil will accurately indicate that your preventative maintenance program doesn't work as it should. The state of a plant's housekeeping can tell you a lot about plant performance and workforce discipline. A good management team will prioritize housekeeping and make it one of their weekly duties.

Housekeeping tours are an approach I suggest and they are a best practice for any operation. The key operating team members should spend an hour a week on a housekeeping tour. Management attention keeps this priority in front of everyone. Notice I said one hour without mention of the size of the operation. It may take all year to walk through an operation spending one hour a week or it may mean that you can cover the entire operation each week. It doesn't matter. The message will be sent and word of mouth will get that message spread throughout the plant. Plus, you do not want to make it a dreaded assignment for the operating team and miss the message. The tour can cover many things simultaneously. Poor maintenance practices, safety items and a lack of discipline in a specific area that are factors in poor performance by a specific team. The tour will also give the tour team a feel for the pulse of the plant. A housekeeping tour will not be effective if, at the end, the results do not get included in a housekeeping metric ranking each area of the plant. These results can be reported at a weekly performance meeting. It has the benefit of setting up a little competition. In one plant I worked in, we had a little trophy for the worst area—of course no one wanted the trophy which was a good motivator.

Safety and Ergonomic Knowledge Pay

Another best practice that has been well documented over the years is safety. Workmen's compensation costs money and not only affects the quality of life of the employees, but can be directly measured in the plant's performance. Do you have a safety team? You should. Safety statistics, such as how many people visited the plant doctor or have requested medical assistance from the outside should be kept, monitored and plotted just like quality statistics. A good safety team will monitor performance and, like the housekeeping team, supplement metrics on medical department visits with routine plant tours to identify unsafe working conditions. They should review all new equipment purchases and sign off along with the engineers before new facilities get shipped to the plant. Additionally, all re-arrangements, shipping containers and material purchases should go through the safety team. Safety teams will look at a piece of manufacturing equipment differently than an engineer. Engineers do not tend to take into account how an individual will interface with a machine. Safety teams, on the other hand, spend a lot of time developing a calibrated eye for safety related design issues which most equipment manufactures do not appreciate or usually consider.

Ergonomics is not the same as safety but related. Ergonomic injuries take time to evolve and occur through repeated motions that an employee may do day in and day out. All ergonomic problems can be dramatically reduced or eliminated if the conditions are understood. Like safety injuries, ergonomic injuries lead to lost time for valued employees. This can also be a cost hit to the operating budget. Ergonomic issues tend to be harder to identify and even harder to supervise. By supervise, I mean that workers will hurt themselves in the long term if they can identify with some short term benefits. For example; assume that the ergonomics team identified that the weight of part could be handled by one average size person, but over time would result in an ergonomic injury. An ergonomically trained process engineer will process the job to require two people to lift the part. Human nature being what it is, however, will lead the two people to soon realize that one person can lift the part and the other can sit and relax or take an unauthorized break. They will set up their own relief system even though they were told to work as a team and not lift the part by themselves. Be assured, this will happen. Over time, and it may take years, both individuals will develop some permanent injury resulting in either medical costs or a reduced quality of life for the individuals. This is a reputation you do not want to have in your plant. The only way to avoid it may be to find a process step whereby this situation does not occur. Ergonomic injuries happen because process engineers and people believe tasks that they are comfortable performing on a limited base can be performed continuously.

Over time, ongoing safety and ergonomic issues will start to haunt you and the plant budget. Companies tend to look at the cost of safety and ergonomics just from the standpoint of worker compensation costs. However, when a injury occurs, there is usually lost production, time spent analyzing the root cause of the injury, and subsequently the costs to fix the problem so injuries do not happen again. It will surprise you how expensive one small injury can get. So again, experience dictates that creating ergonomic and safety teams is a definite best practice.

Operating Patterns Impact Productivity

While not perceived as a critical issue to many managers, operating patterns have a large impact on the quality of life of your employees. As a result, shift preferences should be discussed with employees and addressed in a very serious way. When Henry Ford went to an 8 hour/5 day work week, he forever changed the way the world's normal work week was defined. He made a shift/operating pattern change in his plants and changed the word's work habits, quality of life, and economic drivers everywhere. European manufactures are taking that one step further with 36-39 hour work weeks and a no weekend overtime philosophy. In this case, however, the rest of the world is not following. This may drive manufacturers to slow migration/evolution to build facilities outside of Europe—one of the current trends in "Industrialution". These are examples that dramatize how shift patterns affect economies, employment, and product decisions.

Investment needs are interwoven with shift and operating patterns. In general, if you are heavily invested in equipment, then you must keep those facilities running 24 hours and 7 days a week less downtime for preventative maintenance. This forces you to consider a seven-day, four shift operating pattern. If, however, you have very little investment and your output is based on employees using simple tools, belt conveyors, fixtures, etc., then you will want to work a non-overtime schedule. One shift may be preferable avoiding any type of off shift premium or added supervision for a second shift operation. It may be a benefit to add more employees and low cost tools to one shift versus adding a second as volume/sales dictate increases. There is no general best practice on shifts, operating patterns or start times. It all depends on the industry you are in along with the area of the country and the makeup and attitudes of your workforce. There are, however, some rules of thumb experience has shown covers most of the alternatives:

- 4 shift/7 day operating Pattern—reduces worker stress but requires more workers. More workers require more benefits. A slow down in sales will force layoffs as you have no flexibility in your work force.

- 3 shift/5 day operating pattern and work overtime if necessary—time and a half for overtime may be cheaper than the benefits you are paying your employees, so this could be the low cost approach and give you the flexibility to use overtime to adjust for sales variations. Worker stress could skyrocket if this is an ongoing game plan and after a period of time, workers will establish a quality of life based on the wages received for this overtime. If the overtime stops, workers will, like an alcoholic or smoker, do what it takes to keep on the habit—in a plant that usually means slowing the process down, forcing maintenance where attention could have avoided the need, and other such approaches.

- Facility dictated operating patterns—Steel mills, glassmakers, and chemical processing plants all have one thing in common—they can not afford to shut the facilities down. Glass manufacturers will break the glass at the end of there float glass lines, re-melt it, and run it back through the process when sales fall off to avoid shutting down the furnaces. Shutting down furnaces is these industries is far more costly than scraping parts made from good production. In cases like this, the operating patterns are built in based on the technology and are not open for adjustment.

Experience in operating pattern evaluations over time has convinced me that major concerns will develop over time if manufacturers do not spend enough time on this subject explaining the why and where-fors with their employees. A bigger issue is that if you don't study how to optimize your shift patterns, you will not know if you have or are properly taking advantage of the most cost effective way for utilization of the plant's facilities. It is always interesting that manufacturers will go with the norm for their industry or whatever is the norm in their country or local without looking at alternatives. Understanding that there are alternatives, which could be more productive as technologies and process evolve, could be a win/win for the employees and the plant. Operating patterns need to change with the evolutions in every industry. It has become an integral part of the "Industrialution" experiences. This is why an annual look at operating patterns is a best practice. The world of manufacturing is moving so fast that you must re-visit work patterns often.

Respect Microprocessors and Computers

If a human interacts with an electronic device that handles a lot of data in milliseconds, it is called a computer. If a machine takes instructions from an electronic device it is called a microprocessor. In either case, they have been the biggest change in manufacturing driving the current round of "Industrialution". CAE/CAD/CIM are the buzzwords that interconnect the world of computers, microprocessors, and human information systems in today's manufacturing environment (CAE stands for computer aided engineering, CAD is computer aided design, and CIM is computer integrated manufacturing). It follows that if you understand and can handle a computer, it can be a very valuable tool. However, what is starting to evolve (especially as the computer literate children are growing to adulthood and taking their place in the workforce) is that the world believes that 'knowledge of' and the ability to program and use computers/microprocessors is in itself all that is necessary to makes things happen—in manufacturing this means if you are computer literate you will add value to the workplace. This mindset is dangerous. That is why I believe it has become a best practice to periodically address what your software systems are being used for and who understands the assumptions that went into the algorithms that were developed for the software systems. I don't mean the basic word processing or spreadsheet programs, I mean all the other software programs developed specifically for your equipment and plant operating systems.

Using computers in a manufacturing environment can be a best practice if handled properly or it could be a disaster to a plant or process if the applications are not understood. I believe, as other authors are now starting to preach, that the computer's ability to dramatically increase productivity may have crested and will only be responsible for small opportunities in the future. Efforts in industry today to increase the use of Computer Integrated Manufacturing applications, or CIM, unfortunately has questionable value where it is being applied. Data and information are not the same. You need information to make decisions. The challenge is to identify the critical data from the superfluous information. Increasing the amount of information can have a negative affect. The more you generate, the more you mask the data that is needed for decision making. Computers tied to machine microprocessors are so powerful that they can bury you in data. I am not saying do not use computers, what I am saying is that you must make sure that each application for which you want to use a computer is understood. The thought process that should be part of your best practice criteria is that a plant should only integrate computer or microprocessor applications to increase speed of the applications or increase the speed of the data that is needed.

Information specialists that develop original software programs make decision assumptions that get programmed into their algorithms. With time, new employees not familiar with the original assumptions, replace the original program or user and eventually no one is left that understands the process parameters that were built into the software. The user will no longer understand why they get the results they get and what the ramifications are if they make an error. A lack of understanding the process or system that is built into a plant microprocessor or computerized application is unacceptable in a plant operation. Since the buck stops in manufacturing, the manufacturer must live with everyone's misinterpretations, lack of understanding, etc.

In manufacturing, computers are a tool but they do not have the degree of value as they would in a financial institution. Walk through any plant or office and you will find everyone is working on a computer. What do you think the value is of what these people do with their computers? I suggest you find out. Shut down various programs in the plant's information technology system and ask the individuals using those systems to perform the same task manually. What you want to find out is whether they understand the purpose of the software and what they are doing or if they are just filling in boxes with no knowledge of its purpose. You also want to find out if the system is needed. What I am starting to believe is most of these people are doing tasks without much understanding of what is happening behind the screen and much worse, no knowledge of the assumptions that were made when the computer algorithms were developed. And if that is the case in your plant, there is a good chance there are systems on top of systems and a lot of resources are being tied up generating information no one uses nor does the plant have a need for that information.

If your plant computer is tied into an inventory control system, that usually means that when a shipment leaves the plant, the shipment information is fed into the computer through the bar code reader. If this electronically sends a replacement order to your supplier for replacement material, then there is a value and a very good application for the computer. The computer is doing what it is supposed to do. If, however, the data is not forwarded electronically for further use, then there is no value to the system. Accumulating data and transferring the information to the plant schedulers, suppliers or customers who need to know is a value-added operation and can improve productivity. On the other hand, you might find that the bulk of the performance data that is collected daily by floor personnel and microprocessors have no useful.

Prior to the introduction of computers into manufacturing, it was more difficult and time consuming to get key information from the production floor and more attention was paid to the value of information. Computers have allowed us to slip by that critical analysis and we have all become slaves to the paralysis of the mass of information that is available. Computers can be very valuable when key information is generated quickly and consolidated down to a number that can be fed to another machine or a human—a person or piece of equipment that can react to the information imputed. If you can assure yourself this is the case in your plant, then you have optimized the use of information technology systems.

I want to discuss one example with you from my experiences that demonstrates why I am so concerned with this subject and why understanding your system architecture is a best practice. One of the first misuses of computerized information that I came across related to a coil spring manufacturing. A sharp engineer, at the time this occurred, realized that all dimensions for coil spring designs could be based on the formula for the spring constant. All he had to do was put in the required load and expected travel and develop a computer program. It calculated the wire diameter for the spring, number of coils and pitch between the coils. From this information, the plant could build the tooling to make the spring. He then made a generic blue print drawing of a coil spring. For subsequent spring designs, all the engineers had to do is know the weight the spring had to hold, plug that information into the computer, and get the dimensions. The results could be marked on a generic blueprint and sent off to the manufacture to build the tools.

Years later, the spring manufacturer realized that a large percentage of their tools were identical or at least close enough so that the parts produce were not significantly different. When the design engineers were approach as to why they did not just specify a previous coil spring for the new application, they could not answer the question. The original design engineer, who wrote the algorithm for the computerized spring design, understood the physics and math behind the formula for the spring constant. However, the new engineers evolved into a mechanized design mode. Their function was so automated that they no longer understood the basic principals of coil spring engineering. No one was left from the group that developed the first computer program who understood the engineering and mathematical principles. The current engineering group had become robots—plug in the numbers and release the design.

<u>Supplier Partnerships</u>

The biggest opportunity you have to leverage your plant's knowledge base and get productivity and operating system opportunities is to develop good supplier relationships. This is a concept that seems obvious but rarely is it practiced. Developing supplier partnerships is definitely a best practice.

What constitutes a good supplier? The best way to find out is to take the mirror test. In other words look at yourself. Are you a good partner? Then you can apply this same thought process to your partners. There are traits for good partners and traits for poor ones. In Figure 2, there are some guidelines that can be used for the mirror test.

POOR PARTNERS	GOOD PARTNERS
Do not keep promises	Integrity never compromised
No teamwork	Make fair demands on partners
Negotiate only on price	Focuses on cost as well as quality
Not open to suggestions	Honors partners suggestions as equal
Problems drive punishment, not solutions	Use root cause approach to problems
Uses adversarial relationships	Has collaborative relationships
Will not share information	Two-way communication

Table 2

Good partners have two way communication and you can get into your partner's operating principals for such things as: do they do benchmarking, have long term business goals and productivity plans. In other words, does your suppler partner follow the "Industrialution" Experience Principles put forth in this book? There is one sure thing about a supplier, if they fail, you will fail in all likelihood.

This mirror test, of course, is a check and balance for your team to look inward at your own operation to make sure you are following this best practice of being a good partner to your customer. You would like to be partners with your customers and you want your suppliers to be partners with your plant and not just suppliers.

EP's Story Part #9—Does the Plant Practice Best Practices

If you remember, Bill from human resources just returned from a seminar and one of the topics was a discussion of best practices in a plant. He stopped in Dennis' office to tell him about what he learned and suggested they go over EP's routine. He wanted to decide if EP met the criteria other plants found were important.

Dennis said, "let me summarize what we do and you tell me if that meets the criteria you heard in your seminar.

1. *Every Monday after lunch, one member from each of EP's departments, engineering, material control, human resources, production, etc., will meet at the exit to the cafeteria for a housekeeping and safety tour.*

2. *The weekly housekeeping tour team will pick one area of the plant and identifies items to be addressed. The area production supervisor is held accountable to make sure each item gets resolved and must report to the tour team during the next visit to the area. In this way, we have verification that the safety concern or housekeeping concern has been resolved.*

3. *Once per week, all the plant managers and supervisors will meet for one hour to go over plant performance metrics. During this meeting a summary of safety issues and metrics which have been developed to monitor performance are presented. Charts are located on the wall and each week's performance is recorded in order to keep a running trend on improvement or degradation. The safety metrics we use are something like how many times someone visited the plant nurse for any reason and what was the severity of visit. This is plotted in our conference for reference.*

4. *The systems people (computer department) will report at the weekly meeting on the number of programs and the need for each. Once per month, the system group will shut down one specific software application and identify what the response and value add was lost or not lost. In this way, the systems group will identify needs and what type of training may be needed.*

5. *Also once per month, the quality office will identify the worst supplier and bring that supplier in for a review of proposed improvements. As that supplier improves, the next worst supplier will surface and the process repeated. That way, there will be a continuous iteration of suppliers reporting to our management team on how we can work together to improve the suppliers products and services. A supplier rating system we established identifies the worst supplier. The system was based on the number of rejects in a given time frame and the severity of the reject.*

"Sounds like we have a good system," said Bill. "One thing you haven't discussed, however, and I think we should look at, is the operating patterns in the plant."

"You know," said Dennis, "we are using the same pattern today that was used when the plant opened twenty five years ago. That may just be something we need to do. Set up a special meeting with the operating team and let's look at alternatives. I *will ask George, our industrial engineer, to search out different operating and shift patterns and we can decide if we need to change ours based on today's operating needs."*

"Good idea," said Bill. "I will also get with George to give him some of my ideas."

Key Take Away Thoughts

Championing best practices is like teaching a child to brush their teeth. It has to be taught as critical to day to day functioning. You want these practices to happen automatically. Time management is the most critical resource in a plant environment. You do not want to spend your time on issues that should have been routinely addressed and subsequently monitored. You want to plant the concept of a set of best practices into the mindset of the workers, employees, team members, associates or whatever you call them so that they can spend that value added time when they are in the plant doing productive throughput. Concurrently the operating team should be spending their day planning for future productivity improvements, processes, products, and technologies. Remember:

- Housekeeping tours force discipline; clean plants are more productive

- Safety pays besides being the right thing to do for yourself and your employees

- Ergonomics has long term ramifications; people will hurt themselves if you let them

- Be aware of operating patterns on productivity; address it with your workforce

- Beware of the computer; always assume you do not need another software package or computer and make sure it gets justified from a value add standpoint. The trend to add computers for the sake of computers can bury you with so much information you can not identify the data necessary to run the operation

Experience Principle #10: Stress Drives Lean Manufacturing

Thirty years ago, if a company turned their inventory six or seven times a year, most pundits perceived the plant was doing well. In fact, it was difficult to believe those turn rates could be raised more than a tenth of a point per year. Today, if you are not turning inventory 40-50 times a year, you're not in the ball game. Many of the best companies operate at over 100 turns. How did these companies achieve such drastic inventory reductions? The answer is stress. They stressed their systems using unreal tasks. And why did these companies create this driver? The reason is that reducing the carrying cost of warehouse or in-process inventory (usually 12-15% of the cost of the inventory depending on the prime rate) is only one of the cost opportunities. Inventory hides a lot of inefficiencies; e.g. poor operating practices and quality problems.

Lean manufacturing has become the latest buzz-word when describing this process of inventory reduction. However, in the last few years the meaning of lean manufacturing has developed into many different definitions and means all things to all people. For purposes of this book however, I will stay with the generally perceived definition of 'lean' which is inventory reduction, and how to achieve it. Lean manufacturing means doing anything that is associated with reducing waste in the process. That is easy to say, but to understand what waste is becomes more difficult to define. If you intend to eliminate waste, you must first understand the "why" before you implement the how. Reductions in inventory may not necessarily be the right business decision. In addition, the pundits who preach lean manufacturing, ala inventory reduction, rarely discuss the "how to" and generally concentrate on the concepts. I believe there is only one "how to" approach to achieve a lean manufacturing operation. And the approach is one of a need to create stress in the workforce. That is the only driver that will push the envelope.

How Do You Drive for Lean

You want to reduce inventory to identify you operating problems and the constraints to productive throughput but you do not want to reduce it to a level where you loose all flexibility. Figure 3. illustrates the concept of reducing inventory that is depicted as the water level in a stream. Each rock in the stream represents a constraint in your manufacturing system. The tallest rock is the constraint to throughput.

As the water level drops, which is analogous to reducing inventory, the next tallest rock appears and you can no longer reduce inventory—until you identify ways to eliminate the rock or constraint. The highest rock in the stream is analogous to the biggest problem you have to productive throughput. That is why this simple illustration is so important. Until you lower inventory to that level, it is very difficult to understand the constraints and what is necessary to improve throughput. However, once those rocks appear, it forces you to address each one and cut it down to size to gain improvement. The unfortunate part is that all glory is fleeting. Once you cut down the first rock, the next is just below the surface waiting to surface and you start all over. As each rock appears, they become progressively smaller. This equates to the constraint becoming more painful to address that in turn makes it more difficult to get to and understand the root cause of the constraint (rock). The result is that each constraint becomes harder to remove than the previous one.

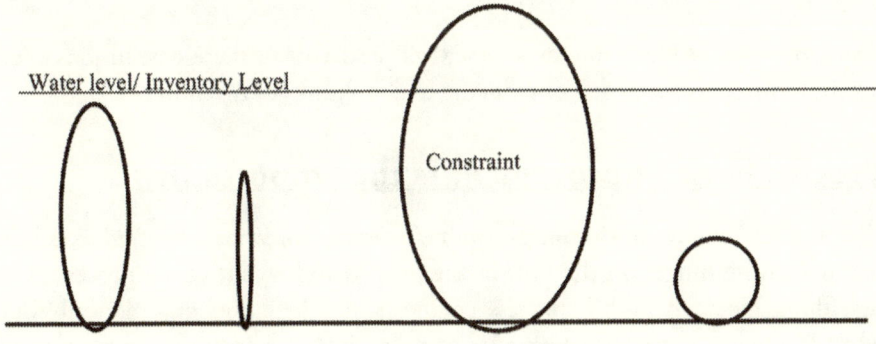

Figure 3.

The pain to remove these constraints will jab you day in and day out until you do something about it. Like any pain the body feels, the immediate reaction is to get to the source of the pain and eliminate it or reduce it to a manageable level. The bad news is that to effectively lower the inventory levels to a point where you feel the pain or stress, it must be self inflected. In other words, in order to strive for continuous improvement you must identify the sources of opportunity, which are the rocks, and force them to surface. And to force them to surface, you must do something physically in the plant procedures or operations.

Why would anyone set up a operating condition that puts pressure on themselves? The answer: it is the only way to drive productivity. Continuous improvement is necessary to survive in today's manufacturing arena and unless you establish a set of conditions that forces you to improve, it is most likely you will continue to operate at the status quo. As we discussed in the introduction, you must provide an atmosphere in a plant operating system that strives for a plant with a future. The key in all of this, and one which we can not determine for you're industry or your plant, is how much pain you create determines how successful you will be. You want to generate enough pressure on the system to get improvement, but do not want to overdo it or you will do just the opposite and put your plant on life support—and that is easy to do. If you lower the inventory levels to drastically, such that all the rocks show, you will not be able to manage your system. Authors who write about the lean manufacturing theory seldom note:

- Reducing inventory requires pain.

- The pain must be self-inflected.

Can I prove this? No. Only experience will lead you to these conclusions. You must live through the agony of reducing major chunks of inventory.

Process Flow Improvement Is the Opportunity

Productivity, inventory control, labor efficiencies, or what is referred to as lean manufacturing hinges on the flow of the process and layout of the process. The first thing most, if not all, process engineers and managers automatically due when laying out a new plant, process or expansion is to identify the location of the biggest pieces of equipment, followed by the smaller facilities. Then, after they locate the major facilities, they work out the material handling issues. This approach, however, is a mistake. Computer simulations and experience will convince you that process and material flow should be developed first, before the location of the major equipment is determined. In fact, the best way to do it is to lay out the material flow and then build the plant around process flow.

For some reason, this is one of the hardest principals to get across to the inexperienced and often even the experienced manufacturing types, most likely because it is a more painful way to address the development of a process. Analysis of current and future process flows seems intuitively obvious to many but we find operating management teams continuously ignore the concepts. Process flow analysis will force you to look at batch vs. cell manufacturing if that fits your type of product. It will also force you to look at your labor cost as a per unity cost, which may or may not be a good measurable. The best approach is to decompose the product design into its manufacturing and assembly elements for processing analysis.

Computer simulation programs have been developed for process development. However, in order to simulate a process, one must address equipment uptime, changeover time if applicable, quality issues, etc. You can lay out equipment in a building or plant site without addressing these items, but you can not simulate process and material flow issues without identifying the root causes of all your potential job stoppers. That may be why it is so difficult to do material flow diagrams before the job is processed. It forces one to do their homework—which in today's society seems to be an irritant (stress riser) more than an opportunity. It takes a lot of up front effort to identify the efficiency of a piece of equipment and a process. But without this information, productive processes will never be achieved.

Getting Started

How do you get started implementing opportunities? Getting started is always the hard part and there are some simple techniques that I have learned that can get you headed down the right path. Let's assume you already work in a plant that is operating day to day and do not have the time or resources to train someone on the hows and purpose of a computerized process simulation program. There is an easy way to find out how your plant layout stacks up and what efficiencies you can take throughout to system to reduce inventory and time. Companies made money and understood the flow of material long before computer simulations were developed. It just took a little more ingenuity.

First, you must identify areas with the biggest potential for improvement. The method I developed over the years is simple and proved to be very effective. It is called the "I am a part" approach. The approach is simple. What you want to do is utilize the services of a new employee—someone who is not familiar with your facility and does not know all the little short cuts in the plant. Start them off by telling them to go out to the receiving dock and announce to whomever is working in that area that "they are a part or material". What they ask the person on the receiving dock is where they go next in the plant, since they are pretending to be a purchased part or some element of raw material. It sounds a little corny but what you want the person to do is to walk to that next location and record the distance they covered. Also, the person must note if there is any value added to the part or material in the process of going to that point. Since a part is dumb and has no mind, it can not make any decisions and neither should the employee doing the study. That is why you want a new employee to do this study. You do not want someone who has been working in the plant for years. They will automatically take shortcuts, and not realize it since they are so familiar with the operation, which means you will miss some of the key information you are seeking. At each point the same question should be asked but it should be noted how long one stays at each location before someone or some automation comes to move that part. The results will be surprising. When the employee charts the results, it will come out something like what is pictured in Figure 4.

Total distance covered : ———————————————————
Value added operations: ——————————
Total time from dock to dock: —————————————————
Time spent adding value: ————————————

Figure 4

If total distance is in feet and the value added operations in feet, then you can calculate the percent of the time you were adding value. The same goes for time. In one of the plants I did this exercise, the building was 900,000 sq. ft. and the total distance covered was three miles as parts crossed the plant three to five times. The percent of time spent adding value to the part was less than 5%. This little approach will quickly highlight where improvements can be made.

Batch Processing Vs. Continuous Throughput

Continuous throughput is simply a batch size of one. The problems are the same. Except when the batch size is one unit, the process comes with more risk and you need to know a lot more about the details. In a batch process, you decouple the individual process operations from each other thereby storing in-process inventory between each of the value added processes. So, how do you decide on batch processing versus continuous? There are three things to consider:

1. The subsequent process steps are so inconsistent that you can not afford to have a continuous throughput system

2. The in-process inventory between the process steps may require a holding period for such things as testing prior to the next step, cool down, etc.

3. Volumes are erratic

Continuous throughput, on the other hand, will require a lot of thought and understanding of the uptime of the equipment, mean time between failures, scrap and rework, etc. Continuous processes are the least labor intensive and, when they are running with a rhythm, are extremely efficient.

There are always tradeoffs between batch and continuous manufacturing which is usually volume or order rates. Understanding your equipment history, process capability, and sales cycles are key to making the right process decisions. If you have gone through the business element thought process described in the first chapter, you should have tools and information available to make these processing decisions. That is why I emphasized that this book is written in a certain sequence. Unless you understand each of the experience principals before you proceed to the next, you will not be able to effectively address or understand why I emphasize the things that I believe are critical to surfing you way through "Industrialution". It puts stress on everyone when you force people to understand all those elements of a plant operation that make for a productive outcome and then apply that knowledge to how they do their job.

Theory of Constraints

Every plant has a constraint. Authors talk about the concepts but rarely, if at all, discuss the "how tos". How do you force the constraint to raise its ugly head or how do you get the rocks to emerge? The answer to the "how to" is to force the constraints to the surface through changes in the plant's procedures and systems that are usually contained in some arbitrary in-house rules. For example; material handling engineers or what you may call the plant logistics group will automatically develop a "dunnage needs analysis" based on some previously developed ratio. Tell them the product and annual volume and they will use their in-house multiplying factor to determine dunnage requirements. Plant engineering and manufacturing engineering or industrial engineering will also do the same thing using pre-determined formulas for cycle times and number of machines per unit of volume, floor space, etc.

This is why it is necessary to force new operating system assumptions. To make these kinds of changes will require stressing the system. You have to:

> **take the pain pill up front by inflicting change in the plant's planning strategy by designing in such changes as reducing the distance between process operations, eliminating the amount of floor space allocated for in process inventory, and/or reduce the number of machines you purchase.**

To get started, it is necessary to change the emphasis by which you drive your operational output. Referring to Figure 5, I will call the driver for the output of the process the drum beat for the process. Depending on how you drive the process will dictate what drives the level of inventory.

Each of the circles is a process step in the manufacturing cycle. The first system is a just-in-case system where the drum beat, or push for production, is at the first step of the operation. You drive the product through the process independent of sales as you make parts based on a forecast of the market needs. The drum is beating at the beginning of the line to release raw materials and/or purchase parts into the plant. It encourages workers to make as much production as possible, regardless of customer's orders. Future throughput is in danger as too large an inventory could cost the plant's budget significantly since you can not predict quality defects and changes in customer's needs and schedules. The cost comes in the form of obsolescence, longer response time to changes, and ultimately higher inventory carrying costs.

The process, pictured in the middle of the figure, exhibits a just-in-time system. In this system, the market pulls parts through the system. You don't start until you have an order. Releasing raw materials and purchased parts into the system will require a chain reaction from the front of the line to the back of the line to get things going. This is definitely a way of getting stress into the system. Now inventory is low, which is what you want. However, every production operation must work if the market demand is to be met. Any disruption in the manufacturing process will cause the entire system to stop, putting your customer and their order in jeopardy. You have created stress by getting everyone's attention. However, it is still not the smartest way or most cost efficient way to operate. It also does not take into consideration that the total amount of throughput in product will be controlled by the system's constraint.

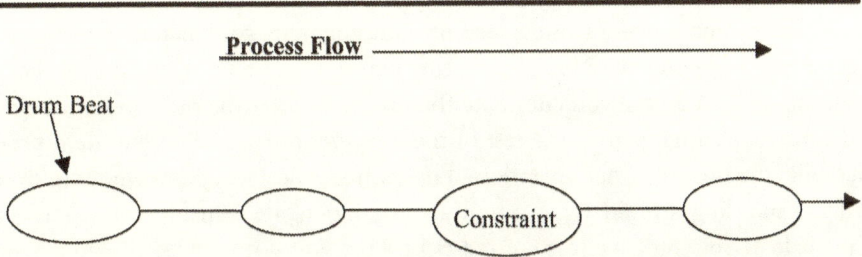

Just-in-Case System - the drum beat is based on excess capacity of the gating operation

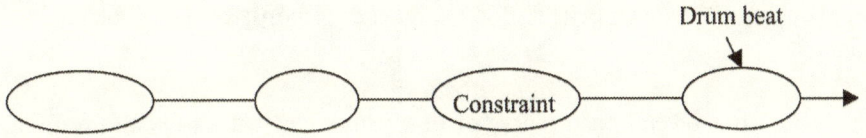

Just -in-Time system - the drum beat is based on marketing demands

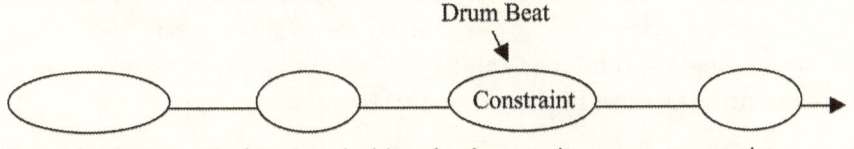

Constraint System - the drum beat is driven by the capacity resource constraint

Figure 5.

In the theory of constraints, there is always one part of a process that will be the bottleneck. You must identify that process step. Verification that you picked the right process step occurs when it is confirmed that every other part of the process can outproduce the bottleneck. Then, you reduce inventory throughout your plant with the exception of the constraint. Ahead of the constraint, you want an in-process buffer of products so that the rest of the line can run when an order comes in so that the constraint is never starved of parts from any other operation. If the constraint is starved, the system can never catch up—and for continuous throughput, you always want the process to run. In this way, you can have downtime in the process steps that are upstream from the constraint and still catch up after they are up and running. Understanding and practicing constraint theory is the best way and the most cost effective way to create stress in your system.

If, for example, the second piece of equipment in your manufacturing line goes down and you have a lot of inventory before it and after it, the process keeps running. Now suppose you eliminate the inventory after the piece of equipment. Of course, what happens is the rest of the line goes down and no end item product will come off the final operation. The entire facility will go down, employees will be standing around (whom you are paying) while valuable manufacturing time is lost. So, you have just created pain. Had you not reduced the floor space and the inventory between your second and third manufacturing operation, you would not have the pain and the rest of the operation would go on producing. Without the pain, you mask the problems and the constraints. The pain created by reducing your inventory will force a quicker response to the problems in the plant.

Than, after several occurrences of downtime, you will do what any human being would do when something becomes constantly painful and that is look for a cure. If masked by inventory, you will not react with the same speed for diligence and that is a cost in profitability. So, what you want to do is create stress to reduce inventory wherever you can, but be smart about it and don't reduce inventory around the constraint. (Note: you may, in fact, have to increase inventory—inventory increases by design are not always bad.)

How Do You Create Stress

How to get started with inventory reduction is a gut call on your part. If you become too aggressive, you can end up putting your plant on life support. This is different than generating pain to force quick reaction to downtime, scrap, and other problems. No facility is up 100% of the time, free of scrap and repairs, or constantly runs at the equipment manufacturer's reported cycle time. What you want to happen is to force your operating people to address these issues as soon as they happen and drive the system to perfection. Response time is the key. The closer you get to optimum performance, more opportunities will arise for new business without added investment and that is the payoff.

How do you self-inflect the pain that creates the pressure to force change? Here is just one approach. Assume you manufacture a product from raw materials, followed by an assembly operation that adds purchased parts to the product manufactured. Prior to the start of production and as part of your facility purchase expenditures, a decision has to be made as to how many in-process storage racks (racks that will sit behind each process step and hold inventory prior to the next process step) you have to buy. If you were to buy a significant number of in-process storage racks, then each individual piece of equipment in the process could run independently of the other without affecting the assembly of the end item, which gets shipped to the customer. When any part of the manufacturing or assembly system goes down for maintenance, every other process operation can continue to run. Now, if you decide to eliminate all in-process racks, all the manufacturing process operations must run at the same time the assembly, operation runs. If any piece of manufacturing equipment breaks down then assembly, as well as the entire process operation, must stop and you can not ship your product. The assembly people must wait while you pay them for idle time. Notice how pain was created long before the process went into production by deciding not to purchase in process storage racks. This pressurized the system. What forced the pressure? Downtime. If the system was set up with unlimited ability to store in process inventory, the operating team would probably never know how often the manufacturing process or assembly process were breaking down. Those little breakdowns, which might only be minutes, add up in a year to major productivity losses. Without a pressurized system, I find that these losses are not recognized. How is it recognized? People are standing around. It becomes obvious and not hidden by the excesses of inventory.

Why create stress and force the issues at all? Because downtime costs money. You may have more manufacturing equipment in the system than you need, and/or you may manufacture in a quality defect and not realize it until assembly, at which time you have generated excessive amounts of scrap. Inventory covers up the root causes of downtime and quality issues. By stressing the system up-front with a decision to keep inventory at a minimum, you also create the opportunity to identify root cause problems much faster.

EP's Story Part #10—Eliminating Constraints in the Process for the New Technology

Dennis, EP's plant manager, realized he had to build stress into his plans so that when EP went into production, it would have a fine tuned highly productive line that maximized utilization of the company's assets for the highest output possible. Theory of constraints is a time based management philosophy that requires the focus of the plant's efforts on the element that has the highest impact on the system's performance. EP will use this approach.

Dennis and DG sat down with DG's entire department for a strategy session on how they would process the new technology and what decision rules they would make relative to inventory, process flow, etc.

Dennis made the first comments. "I would like the team to look at every aspect of the process and I want you to drive for a lean manufacturing system. Minimize the bottlenecks, keep inventory to a minimum, and based on your projected uptime for each piece of equipment, I want you to take a task. In other words, if the manufactures suggest uptime is 80%, I want you to assume 90%."

"Ugh," was DG's first comment. "Excuse me for the interruption, but can we do that if the manufacturer only suggests 80%?"

"The manufacturer most likely uses an average based on historical feedback from his customers," said Dennis. "I expect to put pressure on you folks to beat the average. That is only way we will keep ahead of the competitors."

"Okay," DG said. "George? How do you suggest we get started? You are the industrial engineer and, as you know, we have learned through experience that process flow is the first thing to consider. So, you need to define flow. Then you can place the equipment. All the elements of uptime, cycle time, etc. need to be understood before you start."

"Well, let me discuss an approach I suggest we take," said George." I have been thinking about this problem and came up with five steps.

First we want to decide on the system's weakest link by either calculating loads or getting a consensus of each of the implementing teams projections. We are installing this new technology to insert mold flexible circuit boards in its injection molding machines. The team has a good feel for the cycle time and down time of the machines for conventional molding but no idea of what happens when we have a new device to insert the circuit boards into the molds. Also, no one knows for sure what the scrap level will be. In this case, I suggest a consensus vote of the team that was working on this technology in the skunk works plus what they learned from the benchmarking trips. The process steps ahead of the molding machines and the assembly operation are not new, so our industrial engineering data base has detailed information for the uptime and throughput for these process operations. Of course, I will now add a task to those calculations based on Dennis' new directive.

Based on what I have learned from the skunk works team, instead of adding the electronic chips onto a standard board, the chips must be added onto this flexible circuit which will not necessarily be on a flat surface. The skunk works team identified equipment that is coming into the marketplace. Since this equipment is so new, I doubt that the manufacturers have a good database for uptime. However, Norm, our process engineer for the area, predicts this will not be the constraint initially. From this analysis and our consensus vote on process capability and quality levels, we can now draw a process flow diagram and add cycle times and the projected amount of parts we expect to get through in a given time frame. Since EP has underutilized molding machines, we can estimate how much of the equipment will be fully utilized. If our estimates are off, hopefully we will still have capacity left to fall back on.

Second, we must exploit the areas that are projected to constrain the system's throughput while holding back on in process inventory in the other areas. It must be managed in a way that results in achieving maximum throughput. This is critical as it will dictate the pace of the system. This can be done using several approaches: add a shift in the plant, increase operating time by working through lunch periods with relief people, reduce cycle time, etc. So, to make sure we will get enough parts through the molding operation, we will assume that the most effective operating procedure will be to allow for added personnel to run through lunch periods, shift changes, and mid day breaks. This will optimize the use of our most expensive assets.

Third, since the rate of the process constraint dictates how much product gets built, we can subordinate the rest of the process operations, which tends to go against the mindset of most of the operating people. What this means is we will run some of the process operations slower than the equipment needs to run. The natural mindset is to run all the equipment as fast as possible. However, we do not want to generate in-process inventory that could have quality defects. This means, of course that if the nonconstrained equipment breaks down, it must get priority and get fixed as there is little or no inventory ahead of it or behind it. Here, again, we are creating stress in the system at all the nonconstrained process steps as well as the constrained step.

Fourth, we must elevate the constrained system to give it top priority. In this case, the molding machines must be given key resources to make sure that everything is done to keep this process step on stream. The object will be to eliminate it as the process con-

straint such that the next constraint will emerge. Once that is removed, the next highest rock would emerge and that must be the next process step that gets the priority. In our case, I project that the next constraint will be the process that adds electronic devices to the circuit boards. However, this will be proven out one way or the other after the production system is launched.

Fifth, the iterative process starts. Once the initial constraint is broken, the next one and then the next one must be identified. This is the approach we will use to create stress in the system. There is no rest. Once one battle is won, the next one must be fought. In this way throughput will continuously go up, inventory costs will go down, and capacity will be freed up, hopefully for added sales. As we open up capacity, our operating costs will go down and either more profit will ensue or the cost savings can be passed on to the customer, which will help competitiveness."

"That was quite a mouthfull," said Dennis. "It is obvious that you have thought this through. And I like the way you automatically accepted my task. I think we all understand that without stressing our system, we will never get to continuous improvement. DG, your team has a good plan and I agree with George's approach. You have my concurrence, so you can get going. And one more thing: plant folks like the comfort of inventory in case there is a breakdown. They have one less thing they have to worry about if they have in process inventory protection ahead of and behind each operation. But this is a crutch we, nor anyone in manufacturing, can afford anylonger. Make sure you don't build in a crutch."

Key Take Away Thought

Most books on theory of constraints, lean manufacturing and inventory reduction talk about the benefits but rarely discuss the approaches that are necessary. I believe the only way to get constant improvement in throughput and inventory reduction, and generate capacity without buying new equipment is to stress the system and the people. It usually must be done ahead of time before anyone realizes it is happening. This is why two-year planning is critical. It is at this point where you must create the stress—long before it is felt. You task yourself in all areas of the operating system. But you must be careful not to be to aggressive. For if you build unreasonable stretch, the opposite can happen as people will just stop trying. Human nature is consistent in this area. If you have no hopes of achieving a task, you just don't try. You want to stress/task your system and your people. You don't want to give them heart failure.

Experience Principle #11:
Flexible Workers add Flexible Capacity

What are the real objectives when installing a new process? One is to manufacture a product at the lowest possible cost with the lowest possible investment in a quality way. However, there is a second objective—it is to install a process with the agility and the ability to adapt a manufacturing system for change in a timely manner at minimum cost. To understand why, you may want to go back to the first chapter and re-read the first part of the business section and the first experience principal. The world and our competitors are moving faster every year and if you have a highly automated, costly process that is not readily adaptable to changing market conditions and technologies, you will loose the ability to create a plant with a future. One can find many examples where a company has lost their ability to adapt. The human mind is still the most adaptive element in your processing arsenal and should be used to it fullest—and that is why it is crucial to constantly remind yourself that in today's world of "Industrialution", flexible workers add flexible capacity.

The Kiss Theory

Believe it or not, finding a way <u>not to automate</u> is tougher and in the end is the smart play. This may shock you as many manufacturing gurus believe the theory that manufactures must "<u>Automate or Evaporate</u>". I believe this thesis is outdated and one could support a theory that "<u>You will Evaporate if you Automate</u>". My experience does not support nor do I recommend taking either position. What I do support is taking a devils advocate position which means taking the negative approach towards automation and justifying automation as opposed to what most companies do today and that is to assume automation is the best approach. I have found that the "automate or evaporate" theory has created a force in the manufacturing culture where plants automate for the sake of automation never questioning the effects either in the short term or the long term. They fail to address the alternate approach known as the "KISS Theory"(which stands for **K**eep **I**t **S**imple **S**tupid). Keeping a process simple and still automating is possible. There is such a thing as simple automation. However, once you start to automate it becomes very difficult to keep it simple and still perform the task you desire. Addressing or questioning the need for automation vis-a-vis human intervention necessitates you constantly apply the "KISS" Theory.

To Automate or Not To Automate

Japan Incorporated evolved the concepts of whether to automate or not automate into the follow philosophy:

* *Man—good at Thinking*
* *Machine—Good at Repetition*
* *If Process can be improved to where thinking is eliminated, it is a good candidate for automation.*

The key word in the above philosophy is candidate. The process might be to point that no thinking is required, but with the constant acceleration in change, you still may want to keep flexible workers. It is important to remember that people are your most important resource, not robots. You must always question "why" for each process decision or automation decision in the context of time. Time to react to change which can be answered when one looks at the adaptability of the process being installed.

Automation can cover anything in a plant, from a specific process function in a specific machine to a complete lights out plant. And complete lights-out plants have been built and do operate. They are not just theory. What happens too often, however, is that plant management teams assume automation is the productivity answer to a facility's future without realizing the ramifications of automated systems on changing long term commitments. Automation will box you into the status quo and will not allow a plant to adapt to changing needs.

Today with the ongoing waves of industrial evolution, society is driving manufacture's to thrift time out to respond to every little change in the market place. Time to adjust, to be agile and quick on your feet is becoming more and more the driver to decision making for facility investments. "There has never been a silver bullet in manufacturing to solve the productivity battle," said Frank Ewasyshyn, Chrysler's Vice-President for advanced manufacturing. "If there is a silver bullet, it's a customized operating system that leverages everything—labor, brain power, machinery, computers, waste elimination and capital. Toyota has taught the whole world that." Your workforce is your biggest asset not your automation. For this reason, if no other, the following experience tells us—don't automate unless you have to.

The ultimate tutorial on design for the sake of automation can be viewed by visiting a traditional German manufacturing plant. German engineers love automation and like artists, find beauty in automation. As a result, most German plants I have seen are automated as if investment wasn't an issue. It is unlikely that a German engineer's first thought would be to embrace the KISS concept of manufacturing. The other extreme, to a German engineer's gung-ho automate or bust attitude towards automation, can best be viewed in a Japanese plant. Japanese plant management teams and the people in the plants pride themselves on being able to master a manufacturing system with very simple approaches. That does not mean the Japanese can't design and build world class automation—they can and do. What they do in their plants is question the need before they decide automation is the solution. To visualize this discussion, consider a process where raw materials go into machines and a completed part comes out and must be delivered to an open wire rack container in any random form or location. A engineer's preferred approach, which you would more likely find in a German plant, would be to build a sophisticated walking beam conveyor and deliver the part in a predictable manner, even though the orientation of the part may not be relevant to the next operation. A Japanese engineer on the other hand, would make a very simple system, which could be a piece of sheet metal or plywood to allow the part to free fall. An American engineer would split the difference. All of these approaches are possible from a processing standpoint, but all have very different investment and labor implications. The German engineer might concentrate on automating the process as that would be his mindset. An engineer trained in Japan may make it too simple. The right answer may well be a low cost belt conveyor just to get the part out of the way. Orientation of the part is not important in the end so an effort to keep orientation during the deliver process is not necessary. This example was not invented just to illustrate a point. These situations existed and I have seen them many times. I observed it in a Japanese plants and German plants during benchmarking trips. The trips were made in the same year to different companies, one in Japan and one in Germany, making the same product. These observations are the key outtakes in a benchmarking trip. They signal you on how your competitors think and/or how the cultures of other countries address manufacturing.

Only Flexible Workers Can Address Losses

What I believe becomes one of the bigger drivers for a flexible work force relates to the seven major losses that occur in a manufacturing operation.

> *Breakdowns*—Equipment loss resulting from any equipment malfunction for any reason or cause
> *Set-Up Time Losses*—Time lost resulting from the downtime while the equipment is being prepared to run a different part or is being altered to meet different specifications—the more automation that is involved, the longer the set-up time
> *Start-Up Losses*—Time lost between the time the machine is started and production begins. Furnaces in steel mills and glass plants sometimes take days to get up to heat before you can start production
> *Tooling Losses*—Loss associated with failure of a machine tool or tool wear
> *Speed Losses*—Lost production when a machine or the entire operation is running slower than the ideal speed or cycle time based on what the manufacturer recommended for the machine or the process engineer projects
> *Minor Stoppages*—Miscellaneous things that happen that can add up to major lost production over a year
> *Quality Issues*—This is a defect and or a rework of a production part which does not meet the final outgoing specifications

The key to these seven losses is that they occur in every manufacturing operation no matter what product is manufactured or assembled and issues that only people can address and resolve in a timely manner. The human mind will, without pre-programming, pick up many of the root causes for losses and solve many as they occur without loss of productivity. I once was responsible for a welding operation that was situated near the entry door for the plant. Every time the door was opened for an incoming or outgoing delivery, outside air would blow across the welder. The microprocessor would pick up the temperature change in winter and trip the circuit so it would shut down. In the summer, the door would be left open and dirt would be deposited onto the surface of the part before it was welded. However, an operator working on the line intuitively noted the relationship to weld quality and the door open in a very short period of time. He converted that input into a solution where he would reset the microprocessor in winter and made sure the door stayed closed in summer. The result was very little downtime. When he told the process engineer what was going on, the engineer erected a partial wall in front of the welder to block the air. If this had been a totally automated system, poor welds would randomly show up at the end of the line and/or the microprocessor would periodically shut down the line. By the time the individual responsible to trouble shoot the line arrived, the root cause of the problem, the opening and closing of the outside door, would have been gone. Having a flexible worker vis-a-vis a robot, saved us major warranty issues (bad welds) and downtime costs.

Volume, Product Mix Changes are Guaranteed

One of the unwritten guarantees in manufacturing is that volumes will be totally different than what was planned. And if you make more than one variation of the same product using the same facilities (mix changes), that will also vary dramatically. This is another driver for manufacturing flexibility. The ability to respond to market-driven change with quality products which meet a customers needs in the shortest period of time—flexible workers coupled with agile/adaptable systems which are robust give you that flexibility. There are key categories of manufacturing flexibility which can be defined as:

- Volume/Mix Flexibility—The ability to change the mix of product offerings within existing capacity limitations which includes reasonable supplier flexibility

- Product/Changeover Flexibility—Ability to convert to a new product with minimal investment or costs and changeover losses

Changing a highly automated plant will drive you to gut the facility resulting in heavy changeover losses. The lost production revenues and the cost of unemployment while operators are on layoff can become massive. An "Industrialution" mindset will drive you to flexibility. That mindset must be one that assumes that you do not build in those "anchors" which are the facilities that can not be moved and constrain your adaptability. Achieving flexibility requires a real ongoing discipline for each decision you make.

Flexibility Decision Methodology

There is a two-tier decision hierarchy that needs to be addressed to maintain flexibility. The first tier does not necessarily address flexibility, but will drive the second level of decisions. As you go through each branch in the decision tree, you will have to constantly return to the first item using an iterative process in order to maintain flexibility.

First Tier Decisions

- Product Decisions

- Operational Decisions

- Financial Constraints

- Human Resources—the flexible workforce

- Technology

One must recognize that there is a synergy between all of the above items and if decisions are made in a vacuum, the ability to capitalize on that synergy gets lost. Design for manufacture has become a major drum beat for manufacturers, but, it is still lost on many in the design community.

Once you address this first tier of decisions, you must go down a level of detail to the operating characteristics that must be understood in order to support your flexibility in line with your first tier decisions. So what are the supporting categories for this flexibly and what should you consider? What initiatives should you work on? Below is a summary of some of the major items that should get your mind going. Of course, it will vary by industry.

Second Tier Decisions

Machine tool flexibility—the ability of machines and tooling to produce more than one product or the ability of machines to convert to a new product in a very short period of time

Process flexibility—closely tied to the above, it is the ability for the entire process operation to convert to a new similar type of product in a short period of time

Material flexibility—can the system accommodate several different materials or is it constrained? Bulk handling systems for the chemical and plastics industries have this constraint to flexibility. It becomes a key decision when designing a plant. If your plant is an assembly operation, the decision may be more simple—such as how many fork lift trucks you buy and how much floor space to allocate for incoming materials.

Location flexibility—this was discussed in an earlier chapter

Technology flexibility—this is hard to get your hands on, since you will not know what manufacturing technologies are coming in the future that will disrupt your facility. However, they will come and be totally different than expected. That is why a "what if" discussion prior to buying manufacturing technology coupled with a benchmarking trip is imperative. Having done all that, however, it still becomes a gut call

Expansion flexibility—having at least one wall of the plant with no encumbrances is key to expansion flexibility.

The flexible workforce will give you flexible capacity and that is one of the key experience principals. Once you have installed your facilities and made all the hardware decisions, you can still remain flexible by the type of work patterns you choose. If you work three shift 5 days per week, you have the ability to work overtime on weekends which gives you flexibility. If you are paying time and a half, it may still be the cheapest way to flexibility since you're paying wages but not added benefits. If you chose a 4 shift seven day operating pattern, you optimize the use of the equipment but have nowhere to turn when volumes drop off or if you get an increase in orders. You have to understand your business and cycle of change in sales to make these decisions. Just keep in mind, however, the key is the flexible work force.

Robots have yet to be built that have the flexibility of a "Star Wars Droid". Anyone who has had experience programming robots and machine vision systems will tell you that man has a long way to go before technology gets anywhere close to the flexibility of the human mind. The following quotation is from an article by Mr. Makoto Kawada that has been published in a Japanese accounting journal: "as production concepts changed from standard mass production to diversified small batch production concepts in the 1980's, the disruption between production and accounting systems became conspicuous. Many manufacturers seem to be failing in adopting the new production systems like Just-In-Time manufacturing in both Japan and the U.S. The major reason for this is the theoretical and practical integration of production and accounting has not yet been realized in actual business—the computer itself gives nothing. The importance of human and cultural factors can never be overlooked in actual management. You have to change the mindsets before you change systems. You have to change the mindsets at an individual level." Mr. Kawada wrote this in the 80's, but it is still true. He was writing about the interrelationship between the financial system and the way we produce parts and account for their costs. The same thing could have easily been written about how product systems are processed. The point here is that there are so many constraints in a manufacturing system that you still need the flexibility of the human mind to keep all the little nuances straight, which can't be projected even after a process and product design is frozen. In today's world, no product design is frozen for vary long. The plant has to be agile at adapting to change.

EP's Story Part #11—How Flexible Should the New Process Be

DG decided he had better talk to Harry, the production superintendent, about how flexible he should make the new process. He wanted to add a lot of automation, but something told him he better go slowly.

DG walked into Harry's office and said, "Harry, you were on the benchmarking trip and saw this new technology. How automated do you think we should make our new process?"

"Glad you asked me," said Harry. "Even thought we collected a lot of data, I think we should limit our automation. The molding machines and electronic component insertion equipment should be automated and have microprocessor capability, but that is all. I thought about having a robot insert the flexible circuit boards into the injection molding presses but I decided we should hold off on that program. I know it will take more cycle time and the process will be slower, but we should start with a manual operation. Then if the technology takes off and the volumes go through the roof, we can always add the automation. This way, by having an operator handle most of the operations, we will learn a lot about the process."

"That is kind of the conclusion I was coming to," said DG. "I was thinking about what we heard about in Japan. Man is good at thinking and machine is good at repetition. We will start out with operators and accept the reduced cycle time, and when the operation becomes repetitious, we will add the automation."

"The other thing I thought about," said Harry, "is that if we start with flexible operations vis-a-vis robots, we will keep the process simple. In that way I can get a feel for the constraints."

"I never gave that a thought," said DG. "But you're right. Let's use the more manual approach. I will tell Norm, who is processing the job, to only assume the bare minimum of automation."

Key Take Away Thoughts

You can study the needs for automation versus human intervention to death and put a financial tag on each approach. In the end, however, it is your gut feeling from your previous experiences that will tell you the answer. Of course, if you have a strong finance oriented company, this comes hard. But here again it is an area where the plant team is the only one who know the answers and they must remember the following:

- Keep a process simple

- Always ask yourself if it is wise to automate

- Remember, your best defense against the seven losses is a flexible workforce

- Volume and mix changes are guaranteed; make sure you can be fast on your feet with a workforce that can handle the changes

Just remember these three words—flexibility, flexibility, flexibility. In the next experience principle, we will build on this to show why it is even more important than the discussion we had in this chapter.

Experience Principle #12:
Time Is the Key To the Game

Time is your least adaptive element. With time, you can do almost anything. If you have done a good job of capacitizing your plant and the plant is running at a highly efficient rate, then what you have done is created the inability to shut the facility down and change the process. Time now becomes the enemy you fight. Loss of time is the downside to developing a successful operation.

Time has surfaced as the number one metric in industrialized operations as "Industrialution" progresses. Time for a product to get through a manufacturing cycle: time to receive raw materials and/or purchase parts, time to ship. Market and customer needs both push and pull the need for manufacturing flexibility. The ability of product manufacturing and design to respond in the shortest amount of time to market changes with products that profitably meet customers needs. As defined by the theory of constraints, throughput is the rate at which the system generates money through sales. A product that is manufactured but not sold does not qualify. It merely increases finished inventory. At any given time, your labor costs are fixed and your material costs have been negotiated for a given time frame so the only way left open to improve productivity is to reduce throughput time. And that is how time becomes money.

Time is Money

Your plant must able to change the mix and change the design in increasingly shorter periods of time if you are to continue with productivity improvements and fulfill the needs of an ever changing customer environment. Time is one of our key metrics: the time it takes to make a part, the variation in time from one part or batch to the next, and how long the material stays in your possession. As illustrated in Figure 6, plants must reduce the variations in time to produce each part and reduce the overall process throughput time. Throughput time is the time it takes to manufacture a part or batch. Time affects investment decisions—how long to write-off major facilities. If you purchase a heavily automated manufacturing system, then you need longer times to write off the investment which constrains your ability to change with the environment. The offset is less expensive automation and less expensive usually means more labor and less automation. But labor is the most flexible piece of automation you can acquire (see Chapter 11). You may not have to write it off, but in today's world, the addition of an employee usually means you have that person for his or her working lifetime. So, in many ways you need to look at human assets like they are a fixed cost. The smart play is to weigh investment decisions vis-a-vis the addition of employees. This can only be done after you understand your business and where your plant and product technology is going in the future.

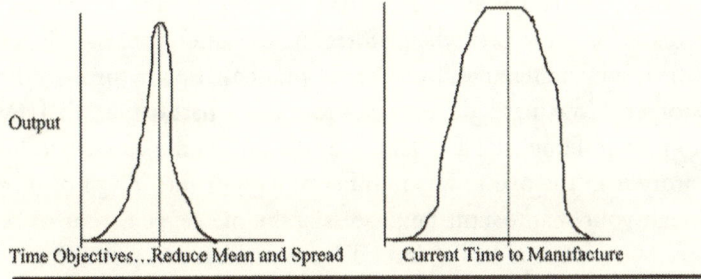

Figure 6

Definition of MTT - Manufacturing Throughput Time

$$MTT = \frac{WIP}{1 \text{ day of Production}}$$

The work in process for a given product you are making or assembling divided by one day of production.

Definition of PTT - Plant Throughput Time

$$PTT = \frac{\text{Total Inventory Dollars by Product}}{1 \text{ Day's Production x Total Cost to Make 1 Part}}$$

The sum of all inventory dollars in the plant associated with a given product divided by the material cost of one day of production.

Figure 7

How Do You Measure Time to Manufacturing

There are two metrics you need to understand: the time to manufacture a product referred to as manufacturing throughput time and the total plant throughput time. Total plant time includes the time incoming parts or materials spend on the receiving dock plus the manufacturing time plus the time finished inventory sits in the plant prior to shipment.

Referring to Figure 7, there are a few simple formulas to calculate time and measure your performance to time. Keep in mind there is no benchmark for time to manufacture.

The objective is to continuously reduce time once you establish a base. The units in the equations in Figure 7 are in days. Depending on your industry, however, you can use hours, weeks, or any other measure of time. Days and fractions of days seems to work the best when addressing the amount of time it takes to get a product from raw material and/or a set of purchased parts through the process to the customer. How many days it takes to make a part is the MTT (Manufacturing throughput Time). PTT (Plant Throughput Time) equates to how many days inventory is in the plant. The number of days or fraction of days it takes to move through your manufacturing process is the metric you want to constantly improve on. Wherever the MTT and PTT are when they are first calculated, the objective is to constantly improve the time it takes to get raw materials and/or purchased parts through the system into finished product and out the door. The faster you push product through your plant, the greater the profit potential and ability to reduce spending. Say you reduce your throughput time by 25%. That means that you just increased you capacity by 25% and if you can sell that capacity you effectively increased your revenue by 25% with zero investment. Time is key and MTT/PTT should be two of the metrics you prioritize in your plant meetings.

Robustness is a Time Metric

The most beneficial time related item to understand when building a production system is the issue of robustness. Robustness addresses the element of uptime and can be handled before equipment is bought or once it is in production. The best time, of course, is to establish your robustness objectives prior to installation of the equipment into the process. In today's environment you will not be able to compete unless you organize for a total commitment to eliminate breakdowns and strive for a 100% robust system. The seven losses in a plant, which were discussed in the previous chapter, must again be emphasized when talking time as a critical resource. You must establish a defense for these losses in order to achieve robustness in your process.

- Breakdowns or Equipment Failures
- Reduced Speed Losses or Reduction in Cycle Time
- Setup and Adjustment Losses
- Idling and Minor Stoppages
- Tooling Losses
- Quality Defects
- Startup Losses

The goal in your quest for robustness is zero breakdowns and zero defects. The approach needed is to organize for total productive maintenance. Total productive maintenance combines the general practice of preventative maintenance found in most American manufacturing plants with the Japanese concepts of total quality control encapsulated around the employees in the form of employee involvement programs. Planning is key. Addressing the reliability and maintainability by introducing a total approach to the subject is the how. And to be successful, there are generally "five hows" which must become part of your mindset:

- Maintenance Prevention by Design
- Individual Equipment Improvement Plans
- Small Dedicated Workgroups for Equipment Improvement
- Predictive Maintenance
- Equipment Quality Assurance

Maintenance procedures and preventative maintenance plans are usually developed by equipment manufacturers. The buying plant, however, must look at it from a standpoint of how the plant plans to utilize the piece of equipment and how it fits into its operating plans. Scheduled downtime periods have to be built into the plant's plans.

Purchase Reliable Equipment

Experience has shown that if you do not purchase reliable equipment and prove it is reliable before it enters your plant, you will never get it reliable. So the first thing you need to do is to make sure the equipment you are buying performs reliability and does the functions and has the capability expected. Runoffs at the equipment manufacture are critical and usually result in time related problems being solved before the item is in your plant and in production. Plant management teams usually assume that a piece of equipment will run the way it is supposed to or the manufacturer will warrant it and make it work. Most likely that is true but what the manufacturer of that facility will not do is pay for your lost production time and the cost of all the resources and inventory which you have on the floor.

The most productive way to check out a new facility is to collect all the individuals who will be held accountable for the performance of that piece of equipment and send them to the equipment manufacturers location to run capability studies. This usually includes the operator, maintenance people and the engineer being held accounted for the purchase of the facility. Many times this may require your employees travel out of the country to the equipment manufacturer's location. The immediate thought is that this can be expense—not only for travel, but for the time out of the plant requiring other employees take their places? The answer is yes. However, my experience has shown that it is well worth the investment. The cost of downtime in most plants is costly and can result in lost business and customers. It takes very little downtime to offset that up-front cost associated with the equipment runoff.

The best way to do equipment runoffs is to manufacture a given amount of product on the equipment manufacturers floor that could be produced in your plant in several hours or several days at a production rate that is at least half of the full cycle time. The quality of the product should be measured, the ergonomic and safety issues addressed and the ongoing capability measured in some manner. Each of the plant representatives should sign off before the final shipment is made. In this way you will know if what you think you're getting is in fact what you will receive. This again is a minor detail in this book but must be mentioned as we have found that these minor details are the items that are usually overlooked and the things that can give you the most trouble.

Additionally, equipment purchase costs must tie to annual maintenance costs to truly understand the cost benefit of buying one piece of equipment versus another. There is no formula or rule of thumb to address this issue. But once again, looking at maintenance prevention from a standpoint of time, time between failures and time to fix the failures is the metric that can trigger the discussion. Nothing is perfect. Equipment will fail and usually it will fail after a period of deterioration. Once a piece of equipment has failed, it usually means it has already cost you substantial losses in productive throughput as it more than likely started to develop intermittent small downtime problems before the failure became obvious. Having a maintenance prevention plan by design that is tied to the purchase of the equipment will be rewarded in the form of the plant's performance and that valuable resource—time.

Workgroups Are Key to Robust and Reliable Facilities

Usually you have an existing set of facilities and must establish individual equipment improvement plans. The most effective way to do this is through the establishment of small dedicated workgroups. The individuals who work around the equipment on a daily basis are the ones that know the issues and problems. These are the individuals who you want for the small work group. They should be the ones that develop the equipment improvement plan and carry it out. This may sound like a simple task and only needs direction. However, just the opposite is true. Most people have to be trained on problem solving techniques, communications, team building skills, etc. In other words, it usually takes a cultural change and cultural changes take time—generally years. So this is no simple task and can not be taken lightly. If properly addressed with a continuing sense of urgency, however, the rewards will be fabulous. If you can successfully keep the same team dedicated to a piece of equipment and train them how to identify and solve problems, the effort will be worth the time it takes to train the small work group.

The use of the word small for the description of the group is intentional. A small work group should only be a few people and is usually made up of the machine operator, maintenance personnel, and the other support persons such as quality control or material handling personnel. If the group becomes too large, it will not be effective. Who has not owned a house, a car, an appliance or a computer that over time developed some problem that required repair? Generally you find you know more about the problem than the repair person. If you do not get frustrated and fix it yourself, you spend a lot of time explaining to the repair person since you know the problem and the symptoms specifically. Without your input, it would be very difficult, if not impossible, to fix the problem. This knowledge is gained since you live in the house, drive the car and use the appliance. Over time you develop a sense of how it sounds, when it is working right or when there are noises or performance problems that are not normal. The same understanding happens with the operator of a piece of equipment in a plant He gets to know the normal sounds and can usually tell when the cycle time is slowing down. With the operator and maintenance people working together, they will see patterns in breakdowns and that means the plant is on its way to predictive maintenance—the ability to predict when a failure will occur. With predictive capability, maintenance can replace parts or make adjustments just before failure is projected and that can usually be done during a time when the equipment is scheduled down for some reason.

The industry that lives by this practice is the airline industry. Can you imagine what would happen if an airline did not schedule maintenance for their airplanes until something failed? Would you fly on such an airline? Yet, how many of you work in or run plants that do not have an intensive predictive maintenance program that is manned by small work groups performing the required preventative tasks before the equipment breaks? Those of you who have not lived inside the four walls of manufacturing and read this would assume this is done as a matter of routine. On the contrary, I would be willing to bet that the majority of manufacturing plants in most countries would fail if audited for a predictive maintenance system.

Studies Verify the Time Metrics

Given you installed an agile system, you assume it is robust and maintain it accordingly. However, the only way to verify this is to do process control studies. A process control study is simply an organized approach to running your manufacturing system for a specific time and measuring, in an organized fashion, all the attribute and variable data generated. There are many books written on designs of experiments that can help you run process control studies. Most proponents suggest using sophisticated experimental approaches. I found, however, that you can easily run studies using some shortcut methods that are sufficient for a manufacturing operation. Usually, manufacturers do not have the time to run detailed experimental studies.

Designed experiments (more recently referred to as six sigma studies) are collections of experimental runs. The runs or tests are conducted to provide information as to how the variables or factors under investigation influence a response of interest. The outcome of the trial (an observation or measurement) is called a response and will vary depending upon the settings or levels of the experimental variables or factors. Appropriately using statistically designed experiments can produce processes that provide high yield and products that do not fail. Such improvements may be characterized by reduction of scrap or rework and improved throughput. If these experiments are designed properly, they can remove inhibitors to high quality and productivity at every stage of the development throughout manufacturing cycle and delivery to the customer. Continuous improvement is an ongoing effort with iterations of the approach noted in figure 8.

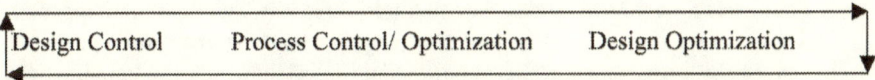

| Design Control | Process Control/ Optimization | Design Optimization |

Figure 8

This philosophy of the continuum in process control and optimization followed by design optimization and process control is a continuing iterative process. Practicing this religiously leads to an understanding of why the revolutions in manufacturing are ever changing. You must learn to drive these evolutions if you are to maintain your competitiveness—there will always be a competitor or some new technology that will be after your business.

This leads to the next logical element of processing called equipment efficiency or EE. Equipment efficiency can be described in a formula:

EE = Uptime x Quality Levels x (Actual cycle time/Planned Cycle Time)

The three elements of efficiency are usually looked at separately and one does not realize that they must be multiplied to get the true reading of productive throughput for a process.

> <u>Uptime</u> assumes the equipment is running continuously during manufacturing hours and does not go down for any reason. Now, in reality equipment breaks down, is shut down for employee breaks, taken down for preventative

maintenance and shut down to change over to another product or process. All this added together takes away from the uptime of the equipment and the efficiency of the investment required to buy that piece of equipment. If you want to run for example 16 hours per day, but must change tools and do preventative maintenance, then your actual uptime is reduced. Assume that it is down 3 hours. Then, your efficiency is 81% or 13 divided by 16 hours.

The second element of the equation is the <u>quality level</u>. If every time the process cycles a good part is made or you get a good batch of material, then your quality level is 100%. If your customer never ships defective batches back to you your quality level is 100%. However, no one or no process is perfect. When you start a process you have startup scrap, there may be by-products of your process, or your customer may just not like the way your product feels or looks and decides to reject the output. If this happens 5% of the time, your quality efficiency level is 95%.

The third element of the equation is the <u>cycle time affects</u>. The equipment manufacturer and your processing engineers estimate should be able to project your cycle time for the process. For all kinds of reasons, that does not happen. Temperature may affect that run time, equipment wear may force you to reduce the cycle, operator ergonomics could affect how fast the equipment runs, etc. Again add up the number of cycles a piece of equipment or process should run over a period of time and divide it by the number you expect it to run and this will be your efficiency level. For purposes of this discussion, let us say that the process cycle time is 98%.

Now we can calculate EE or equipment efficiency.

$$\text{EE} = 0.81 \times 0.95 \times 0.98 = 0.75 \text{ or } 75\% \text{ Efficiency}$$

You can see the effect on throughput. This means that on any given day on the average you will only get 75% of the raw materials and purchased parts through your process to make a saleable part. The remaining 25% will be waste in the form of paying employees without getting a return, and if business is good and expanding, you will be required to fund more investment than necessary to get the product out. If you know the EEs for all the equipment and processes in your plant, you can then understand and determine the constraints in your system that affect adding throughput. They are:

- Cycle Time Constraint

- Down Time Constraints

- Scrap Rates

- Starvation of the Constraint

- Blockage of the Constraint

- Scrap Going into the Constraint

- Scrap Generated after the Constraint

The word "Constraint", as discussed in the last chapter, refers to whatever process or piece of equipment stops you from getting more output. Once identified that the efficiency of the constraint is the only thing worth working on—improving the efficiency of a facility upstream from the constraint does not do much good if it gets held up at the constraint.

Adaptive Feedback—The Next "In" Methods Improvement

Once you develop a true understanding of your processes and can practice predictive maintenance, your ultimate goal is to achieve an adaptive feedback manufacturing system. Obviously, if you can predict when a process will change or a downtime issue will occur, that has to be your best time improvement mechanism. Adaptive processes require a predictive measurement system that can adjust your operating parameters instantaneously based on the upstream conditions predicting what the effects will be downstream. You want to take all the knowledge you gained, put it into some kind of expert system, attach some statistical projections to that data, and tie it to the process, such that adjustments will be made automatically. Adaptive manufacturing systems are one of the waves coming in the future that will drive this ongoing evolution and the way we will run plants. To date, however, I have seen very few examples of adaptive manufacturing systems.

A good example of what I mean by adaptive can better be described by looking at today's automobile engines. In the seventies, engines had carburetors and the vacuum generated inside the engine sucked in the air for the air/fuel compression. If the amount of air changed pressure due to changing barometer readings, the engine had no way of knowing and the engines efficiency changed as it had no way of dealing with ambient air changes. Today, however, vehicles have engine microprocessors that take information form various sensors and feedback that information to the engine management system. There are sensors that measure the incoming air that gets fed back to the engine control. The engine control microprocessor in turn sends a signal to fuel injectors to adjust the air/fuel ratio for the next power stroke of the engine. If the inlet air changes for whatever reason, the mass air flow sensor picks that information up and sends a signal to the engine control. Likewise, sensors measure crankshaft rotation and engine emissions. All of these signals interface with each other, forming a decision matrix based on the algorithms designed into the microprocessor. With this information, the operating parameters of the engine can be changed and efficiency maintained.

A manufacturing process can work much the same way. Heat and humidity affect most manufacturing systems no matter what you make. Given a good history with good data, your small work groups should be able to start making adjustments early in the process before quality problems and/or downtime occurs. Here is when a computer on the manufacturing floor can be very beneficial. Adaptive feedback manufacturing processes are becoming part of the newest wave of "Industrialution" and one which most pundits have yet to write about. To apply it, however, you must understand your process in detail.

EP's Story Part # 12—Time to Produce Must be Minimized

EP is buying new equipment to insert flexible circuits into an injection molding machine. The expense of this equipment requires EP buy as little capacity as possible and in the process, make sure they optimize the uptime. So, they will optimize for a lean approach and to do this, they decide they will stress the process as part of their plans. EP will elect to run the equipment around the clock, seven days a week, and use a workforce that can keep the equipment up and running. Therefore, they will not totally automate the equipment, but keep operators on each molding machine who are trained to not only handle the part to part production, but fix the little problems that may occur with the microprocessor that runs the machine.

DG discussed the assumptions in one of his staff meetings with George, his industrial engineer, and Norm who was the process engineer assigned to this job.

DG said, "the decisions relating to operating objectives that I want to make up front include the following:

- *Uptime—assume 3 hours downtime in every 24 hours or 87.5%*

- *Quality—98% good parts*

- *Cycle Time—assume the equipment will run to 100% of the manufacturers specification*

With these numbers, the equipment efficiency will be:

$$EE = .875 \times .98 \times 1.00 = 85.7\% \text{ or } 20.5 \text{ hours output per day.}$$

Do both of you agree?"

George said, "based on the manufacturer's cycle time and the volume, we must get per year, I can calculate the number of machines we need. But we can't forget maintenance downtime. If you agree to letting the plant shut down every 4th Sunday DG, then I will agree with your assumptions. But to protect my calculations, I want to be at the equipment runoff and have veto power if the equipment does not support the uptime numbers you propose."

"I don't have a problem with either of your wants," said DG. "So let's decide that on every 4th Sunday, the plant will be shut down from production and the equipment will be worked on based on, the preventative program Norm develops with the equipment manufacturer."

Norm challenged the 4th Sunday downtime plan saying, "I have been here long enough to know that when sales wants product, we will bend and run. So I don't buy the concept."

"Well, our plant manager is going to have to take a stand on this one since we have never before facilitized for a seven day round the clock operating pattern. That will be his problem and why he is getting paid the big bucks. We talked about this and he and I concurred. So don't worry about it, Norm, you have enough other people to fight with."

"Okay," said Norm. "then my plan has to includes experimental studies ahead of time to make us confident all of these assumptions will happen. We will do runoffs at the supplier's before the equipment is brought into the plant and make sure the numbers we projected can be achieved. I will require, and write it into the purchase order, a 48 hour run using EP's operators with George keeping track of the uptime. George will be our go/no-go decision-maker on buying before the equipment is shipped to EP. With this run, EP can then calculate the manufacturing throughput time and be able to predict thee inventory levels. This, of course, goes back to the decisions that were made on the quality levels, how much startup scrap and ongoing repairs would be gen-

erated, plus how much time would be allocated to keep the equipment up and run-
ning."

"That is acceptable," said DG. "But there is one other thing. I want to establish a
PTT time of two days and a MTT of one day. I know that is aggressive, but that has
to be our objective."

"You will really stress the system," said George. "But I guess we know that it is the
only way we are going to stay competitive."

"Only one small comment," said Norm. "You told us time is the key to the
game. You didn't say no time is the key—only kidding, I'm on my way. I know what
I have to do."

"Believe me," said DG. "That is the way I feel most of time—if I had the time."

Key Take Away Thoughts

Time is the key to the game in today's world of "Industrialution". It is not
easy to understand, however, the underpinnings of time. The how-to is what is
difficult to comprehend and implement. Remember:

- Time Is Money
- Measure Time Using MTT and PTT
- Robustness Is Time
- Purchase Reliable Equipment
- Workgroups Are Critical
- Equipment Efficiency Must Be Understood
- Monitor the Seven Losses

These are keys to time management. Your time elements—the underpinnings
that will make you successful.

If you read the book that Tom Clancy and General Fred Franks wrote on the
Gulf War you will find that General Franks spent a good amount of time strategizing on the moves he would make day by day as the war progressed. He had
several alternate plans if it became apparent that the course taken would not
work. Surfing your way through the day by day decisions in manufacturing is no
different than the way a chess master, field general or pool player must operate to
be successful. This mindset must likewise be institutionalized inside the culture
of a plant. A manufacturer must anticipate what technologies, volumes or other

changes could happen and what the affects might be on the ability of the processes and people to adapt in a timely manor. Time is the biggest enemy at staying the course and maintaining a plant with a viable future. So, make sure you have moves planned well ahead of time.

Experience Principle #13: Wisdom is Quality

"Quality is a given or The customer is king." These are typical of the quality mindset in most operations. And it is a mindset that every company must have. Whatever your product and wherever you sell that product, the quality evolution will never let up. It has become a given that if you want to stay in business, the quality and durability of your product is critical. Either produce a quality part or you're not long for the business world. I believe most everyone understands that in today's environment, but not every plant operation achieves acceptable quality levels, even when they perceive that they do. It happens for two reasons:

- What you say you do to control quality is not what you do
- Your perception of a quality product is not the customer's perception

Companies spend a lot of time and money controlling tolerances, specifications and visual appearance in areas their customers do not perceive as important. When they do identify what is important, they do not always convert that definition of quality to a metric or procedure that is monitored and tracked. Manufacturing plants tend to expend a lot of their effort on controls and procedures that their internal operating system (bureaucracy) believe is important. They get trapped with specifications that were developed in the past for designs and materials no longer being used, or requirements that are developed internally without relating to customer needs. It takes wisdom to convert the customer needs to plant specifications and controls. This is why I have dedicated a chapter in this book to the concept that "wisdom is quality".

The Evolution of the Quality Paradigm

The quality of products manufactured in the early 50's, by today's standards, was junk. After the Second World War, manufacturing was at an all-time growth rate but with little regard for the quality or long term durability of a product.

150

When Japan started to rebuild and came into the modern day industrial world, their products were so bad that they made the rest of the worlds output look like high quality in comparison. Japan's manufacturing output was universally referred to as "cheap". But Japan Incorporated soon realized that such an image could not continue if the country intended to re-build its economy. They needed to change the mindset of every employee in every company. Japan's corporations wanted their employees to have wisdom when it came to understanding quality standards. They deemed that this was necessary if the country was to change their image from one who produced cheap products to that of one who produced quality products.

Subsequently, they (Japan's industrial complex) invited American Edwards Deming to come to Japan and teach them the theories of waste and quality control. Deming engrained into their society a passion for quality. This passion for quality drove the Japanese economy into a modern day industrial giant and eventually changed the rest of the world's outlook on what quality was and why it is so important. What evolved was obvious—obvious being that it affected the market share of the global competitors of Japanese companies. It was the start of a quality tidal wave that erupted in the east and moved west where it continues to roll without loosing momentum. Deming was so successful that Japan instituted the Deming Award, which was presented to companies each year that demonstrated the cultural change in quality principals outlined by the government.

Many non-Asian industrial managers believed that there was something in the Asian culture that allowed or fostered this ability of the Japanese to work together and gain the upper hand in quality procedures. This mindset, however, is further from the truth than one would believe. Many years ago, I attended a seminar in Washington D.C. sponsored by the Japanese/American Institute on Japanese business practices. One of the speakers was a Japanese American citizen who had grown up in America. As a teenager, he was sent back to Japan by his parents to get educated in the Japanese culture. He arrived in Japan a month before Pearl Harbor and the start of the Second World War.

He went to work in an industrial concern and when the war broke out was stuck in that plant for the duration of the war. The plant he worked in was converted to war production and he was destined to work in a facility that made war material. His daily work routine in that environment is the point of interest. Each day he and his cohorts would look for an excuse to get out of work. When the boss wasn't looking, they would sit behind a heat treating furnace and smoke cigarettes and discuss the social scene and how they would spend the evening. The object of their day was to spend as little time as possible working and as much time as they could goofing off and looking for excuses not to be productive. In his case, he obviously had no desire to get production out the door. But his fellow workers, who were born and raised in Japan, also did not care. You would have thought that they would have been operating on overdrive for the good of the country. In fact, they were operating no differently than many employees operate today in an industrial plant where, in their mind, there is no connection between their effort and the output of the company—let alone the ultimate result of the war. This was the mindset of the Japanese industrial workers pre-WWII.

This does not sound like the Japan many visited, benchmarked and wrote about. The mindset of most benchmarkers that evolved in the 70's was that this culture always existed. This Japanese/American professor's point, however, was just the opposite. The quality effort and the drive for continuous improvement that is characteristic of Japan is not a cultural trait developed over generations or the result of some other inherent microcosm in the drinking water. The work ethic embedded in Japan's culture was nurtured over time. That is why Japan had the reputation of making junk in the 50's. By the late 70's, that image had changed. It changed through hard work and a commitment by the country as a whole and the Japanese corporations to change their quality image. If a plant does not have quality ingrained into its mindset and everyday practices, there is no cultural reason why it can't be done. However, it will take time—years not days or months. A time commitment that must focus on changing the quality culture is necessary.

Who Defines Quality

A relatively simple question when stated becomes very complex when put into practice. Putting the definition of quality into practice means defining quality in some sort of metric. (Note: a metric is a qualitative way of measuring a product such that when manufacturing perceives the product is acceptable, it is acceptable to the customer. The customer has the same perception) So, your first thought may be to ask the customer. However, you can not ask you customer until you know who the customer is. There are several customers (we discussed who they are earlier in this book) each with different perspectives on what is quality and what isn't a concern. And their definitions may not jive with each other. So, your customers are many and all their needs must be addressed.

Once you have your customers identified, a needs analysis must be done. This takes some ingenuity. For example; when the Japanese first started shipping cheap parts to the rest of the world, it coincided with the evolution of the plastics industry. So, many of their products in the early 50's were plastic and what has become know as cheap plastic. In those days, the molds they used were smoothly finished which resulted in a shiny part. Over time, customers worldwide began to believe that a shiny plastic part was cheap even if it was made out of the most expensive plastic known to the industry. Many manufacturers found this out over time. The solution? Grain the surface of your mold such that the plastic has a grainy look like leather. Customers perceived this as expensive. Did this cost more? No. In fact, the grain hides surface defects and, in general, you can get away with less scrap and use a lower cost plastic. The end product is a more highly perceived quality part that, in fact, could be a cheaper product.

The message I want to convey with these two examples is that quality doesn't mean increasing cost. It means wisdom is needed to understand a customers needs. Customers define quality based on perceptions not on the reality of what is more costly or time consuming to produce. These perceptions can be contrary to your mindset and to the cost of manufacturing a product, which makes it hard to understand. Living in a manufacturing operation, you are close to the day to day issues that sensitize your perceptions. The more you know about the specific product details, the more you tend to see defects that a customer doesn't see. As a result, it usually requires some unique marketing techniques to get to what your customer perceives as quality. That is why "wisdom is quality" is an experience principal, meaning it is a principal that one must spend a lot of time understanding.

What You Say Is What You Do

Success in the quality arena is achieved when you can honestly say, and prove through unbiased audits, that "what you say you do to promote and sustain a quality operation is what you do". Or in other words, you define what it takes to produce a quality part and insert that definition into the required checks and balances, along with all the necessary metrics to make sure it happens on a consistent basis. I would think that most plant operating teams believe this tie of field expectations and performance to manufacturing controls has always existed and everyone has a system. Unfortunately, this isn't the case and the reason that the ISO 9000 requirements have been gaining momentum around the world.

A good quality audit will always turn up procedures that aren't being followed or quality concerns that were not addressed. If you can understand and accept this, then you can go about changing the quality culture. Changing the culture requires a good quality system. This means documentation and structure. There are four levels of documentation needed to make up the structure and documentation required for a good quality system:

1st Level—The Quality Manual: these are policies and objectives. What the plant wishes to achieve. Answer the question, why does the plant exist—what is its role?

2nd Level—Procedures: how your plant or company implements its policy structured to reflect process flow of events.

3rd Level—Work Instructions: detailed instructions on how to complete a job or task such as machine instructions, computer imputes, etc.

4th Level—Technical Data: interpretation standards if appropriate, detailed product specifications, computer operating manuals, etc.

Most plants have these levels of documentation and procedures. The hard part is to make sure they all tie together. That is the challenge. For instance: the level one quality manual may make a statement that the plant has an inspection and test method for <u>every</u> part or batch. The word <u>every</u> means just that—<u>every</u>. So you have to make sure that every last end item part or batch has a test. If they don't, or testing is not required on every part or batch, you can't say every. Notice I said end item. However, the word part was not defined as end item. So somewhere the word part or batch must be defined.

Having done that, the next level relates to procedures. Does every part tested have a procedure? The answer must be yes. Plus, there has to be a work instruction on how to follow that procedure. If every part is tested and has a procedure for testing, then there must be a work instruction on how to run the test. The work instruction must refer to level four or the technical data that defines the test equipment and the detailed product information. So you see, what starts out as a simple statement gets involved. And what makes it more complicated, is that most procedures, work instructions or technical data get referenced in other procedures. Suppose that, buried in level four, there is a reference to a test requirement that the development engineers are required to perform. Then, you as the manufacturer must include a tracking system that makes sure the product engineers do the testing and the results are recorded. Why do you have to worry about the requirements of some other function? Because the buck stops in manufacturing. Remember, manufacturing is always ultimately responsible.

Listed below are the elements of a good quality system. These elements must be ingrained in the culture of every employee so that an outside auditor can come in and be convinced that your location has a quality mindset. A good system contains procedures written for each of the elements including work instructions describing who performs the function:

1. Management Responsibility

2. The General Quality System

3. Quality Planning System

4. Contracts and How They Are Reviewed

5. Control of Design Changes

6. Document and Data Control

7. Purchasing Procedures

8. Control of Customer Supplied Parts

9. Traceability and Product Identification

10. Process Control Procedures

11. Inspection and Testing Methods, Procedures, Tracking

12. Measurement and Control of Measurement Equipment

13. Control of Non-Conforming Parts

14. Corrective and Preventative Action

15. Handling, Storage, Packaging, and Delivery

16. Control of Quality Records

17. Internal Audits to Verify Conformance

18. Training

19. Servicing

20. Statistical Techniques

21. Approval Process for New Products

22. Continuous Improvement Programs

23. Manufacturing Capabilities

Figure 9

The process of going through each element in a detailed way will eventually lead to thorough understanding of the plant and the operations in the plant. It is important to remember that this document should be a value-added document. Each element must have a purpose, scope of responsibility and supporting level of procedures.

This will be painful, but if it is not painful, it will not be successful. I can not emphasis enough how important it is to write everything down and define each word to make sure you understand and your people understand. Tom Clancy wrote in one of his novels, "if you did not write it down it didn't happen". In a manufacturing environment, this concept can be slightly modify to say—if you do not write it down, it won't happen. This is wisdom you gain with experience.

Setting Up the Quality System

So how do you go about developing your quality manual and work instructions? First you must assign an element champion for each of the element items I noted earlier. Once that is done, each champion should walk through a disciplined approach to writing up his or her element. These write-ups or critiques will be put into the quality manual. When all the critiques are written and approved by the plant's operating team, the plant has a quality manual. A mechanism to develop these critiques in a disciplined approach is needed. I have found the following works:

1. Develop a flow chart of the current system as it applies to each element

2. Review and interpret the requirements of the element

3. Develop a flow chart of the current system that is in place

4. Review and interpret the element

5. Write a draft of the element as it is currently is practiced

6. Compare the draft to what you think is required

7. List the gaps that exist between what you think it is and what it is

8. Check with corporate procedures for consistency

9. Revise the element with the management team or a committee

10. If it is accepted, insert the element write-up in your Quality Manual

After you have written a procedure for each of the elements in your system and combined them into a manual, you have started on the road to having a true quality system. Now when your customers ask how you manage quality, you have a system to present. By writing it down you force yourself to answer these four questions:

1. How do you manage quality?

2. Is there a system and is it internally consistent with everything you do?

3. Do your employees understand the policy, procedures, and the system?

4. Do you do what you say you do?

Quality assurance is defined as "all those planned and systematic actions necessary to provide adequate confidence that a product or service will satisfy given requirements for quality". Customers require you to have a set of rules and follow the rule book. Having a quality manual verifies that you do. And this must be your own at your local plant site. A corporate manual that is generic in nature will not do. You must have one specifically designed for the things you do at your location and it must be consistent with your business policy and the definition of who you are as defined in the first chapter of this book.

The Audit

Having completed your paperwork and documented the plant's needs and procedures you now need auditors. If you don't audit the system, how do you know if the system is being followed and employees understand the system?. Therefore, over various time frames, a plant needs to bring in outside auditors who will be totally unbiased and verify that the system is totally consistent with what you say is what you do. However, you don't want surprises, so that requires each operation develop their own internal auditors. They are individuals who have a regular job in the plant but are trained in the quality system.

Periodically, meaning every six months at the most, they should randomly audit the procedures and tests to verify they meet the intent of the quality system. For every item they find that does not meet the procedures, the auditors should prepare an action form that can be called a non-conformance notice. It should be presented to the operating team along with instructions to clear up the non-conformance within some limited time frame, such as 72 hours. Why? Because you need to have a sense of urgency associated with any and all non-conformities sending a signal to the troops that this will not be tolerated and must be addressed at once. In other words, stress the system. This is a discipline that becomes grueling over time, but is necessary as the importance of polices and procedures have a way of being downplayed over time.

Six Sigma and other Quality Metrics

Useable metrics are needed by every good manufacturer. Metrics are necessary that make reference to anything you need to know about in a process. In today's society quality is a given, which means manufacturing must deliver. Since nothing in this world is perfect, no one can design and build the perfect product. Therefore, a plant needs to define a set of metrics which, in the plants mind and its customer's mind, equates to zero defects. The perception of quality, unfortunately, is one that is usually lost as individuals spend more and more time in a plant. They get sensitized to discrepancies that customers don't view as discrepancies. As a result, fruitless hours are spent improving some characteristic or performance standard about which no one cares. They evolve to spending company money and time on non value added effort which could be used on more profitable endeavors.

You can and should shoot for zero defects, but you must realize that you have to set some target for your factory to run to if you expect to ship product. So, where do you start? Some authors have stated that 99% is a safe bet. Sounds good doesn't it? But think about it. Based on statistical studies from a few years back, if 99% was an objective, that would mean 20,000 lost articles of mail per hour, unsafe drinking water almost 15 minutes of every day, 5,000 incorrect surgical operations per week and 200,000 wrong drug prescriptions each year. Knowing this, who of us would believe that 99% is good enough? Obviously no one. So, where do you start if 99% is too low and zero defects, or 100%, is not attainable in the real world? There is no answer, but our experience and the trend over the last few years indicates that six sigma quality levels or 34 PPM (34 parts per million or 99.999966%) is needed to get you into the ballpark. Anything less is not acceptable for any industry and improving over 34 PPM is where you must be to stay in business while you try to improve. Without information on your industry or plant operation, I believe the following statement is appropriate: *to play the game of manufacturing you must fully comprehend your customers perceptions of quality and expectations for long term durability and make sure you establish metrics to measure those requirements. Having established those requirements, your operation should only ship products that exceed a 34 PPM or a six sigma level quality level.*

Understanding and building quality into a product requires statistical methods. All stages of activity from concept to the customer must be followed with statistical studies using designed statistical experiments that focus on learning what variables affect the outcome of the process. These experiments play a central role in helping the perceptive observer identify naturally occurring events that affect quality. Many companies are now starting to push a program called the "Six Sigma" program. The programs requires "DOEs" (Design of Experiments) and many companies now carry statistically knowledgeable people on their staffs just to promote, teach, and set up experiments that give a plant team understanding of the variables in their operations.

Designed experiments (DOEs) probe into the processes. Through a carefully planned strategy, DOEs introduce occurrences of informative events that can lead you to understand what affects the quality output of product versus the items that are noise in the system. Variation exists in all processes that could be caused by measurement error or actual variation. Your need to find out why. You must judge the importance of the signals you receive from the experimental model you build and screen out all the noise from the experiment that is variation which does not affect the output of the product. This noise usually creeps into the mindset of a plant's operating personnel over time. It becomes very real from the standpoint that plant personnel believe the product is defective and could cause warranty issues. They scrap or re-work a product that is acceptable. Redoing designs of experiments or "DOEs" every so often will help with the paradigm shifts in the operating teams thinking.

The deeper you get into statistical process control and the more you learn about your process, the more you find you don't know. As a result, more tests are run and more information is collected. At some point, however, the amount of information gets too large or detailed to form a conclusion. In this case, the best rule becomes wisdom. Sometimes you must put aside all that data and information which permeates that great super computer we call the human brain and summarize what you have collected into some type of format that can be understood and converted to a metric.

EP's Story Part #13—The Quality System

A problem EP had to address is that major initiative came down as mandatory from their parent corporate offices—they want to apply for the Malcolm Baldridge Quality Award. And this had to be accomplished in the same time frame in which EP was projecting to integrate the new technology——or at least this was the plants strategy plan and major initiative for the next few years.

Having heard the news, Dennis called his operating team together. "Well, team," said Dennis, "just when we have spent most of the year getting everyone lined up to integrate the new technology, added a skunk works and all the related effort, we now have a new quality initiative which could tie up everyone in the plant. So, I am open for ideas."

Vito responded. "Since I am the quality czar, I guess it is my initiative to quarterback. DG has to integrate equipment for the new technology and I have this one. But I will need help from all of you."

"Why do you need our help to address this quality initiative?" Asked Mary.

"A quality system means we are totally consistent within the entire plant. So if we say we do something, then all the procedures must follow. For instance, we have a scrap tag procedure. And who audits that? Your finance department does, Mary. It is your responsibility to make sure all scrap and scrap tags are accounted for. So, that is your part of the quality system."

"Which means," Mary commented, "my office is probably the best place to verify we have a scrap procedure and that it is being followed."

"I am starting to see where this is all going," said Barb. "As the logistics manager, I am responsible for inventory controls and therefore I have to make sure that there is a good clean procedure on inventory controls and it is in writing."

"Not only that it is in writing," said Vito, "but that everyone is trained and understands the procedure. Which means you will have to audit the system when it is done.

"Which I assume means I need to develop auditors," said Barb.

Dennis stopped the open dialogue session saying, "okay. I am starting to see what Vito meant when he said he would need help from everyone. If we use everyone in the plant, it will spread out the workload and maybe we can accomplish all our actions. I was really down when this memo came through. I didn't know how we were going to get all of our initiatives accomplished—and all means bringing in the new technology, going for a quality award and staying open for business—which says we still have to ship parts during the interim."

"If we move forward on implementing the requirements necessary to get the award, it will require changing the culture and mindset of EP's employees which means training, budget overruns, etc.," noted Vito. "We will have to squeeze in training sessions during regular production hours.

"And there is nothing harder than trying to force mindset changes," said Bill. "Normally it takes years, but I can see we don't have years."

"Well, maybe a few, anyway," Vito said.

"Wonderful," Mary injected. "I did not have any of this off standard operating costs that you're talking about in my budget for this year. Maybe we ought to refuse going for the quality award—if we can"

Dennis said, "we can't. The game here, then, is to not refuse but to put things in focus. When our parent company goes for a quality award or a quality rating like ISO 9000, that means each of the company's plants and staffs must meet the criteria. So, we really don't have a choice. However, one way to handle this is to play the game. Remember when we talked about that, Mary? You need to get together with Vito and Bill and construct a cost chart noting the required incremental resources and extended overtime, along with a projection that the plant will not meet the budget. Add a note that cash flow will go negative. In other words, we will present a positive proposal, but one which will identify the effect on the corporate purse strings. Awards are nice, but I have found they do not necessarily mean we have achieved or will be perceived as having better quality in the eyes of our customer. Wisdom is quality means just that. We must meet the expectations of the ultimate customer, which is not necessarily the same as satisfying the paperwork jungle our plant will have to go through to achieve this quality award."

"I think that is why a lot of companies aren't going after some of these awards," said Vito. "However, like you said, we have no choice, so I need to get going. To get started, I suggest we use everyone in the plant. Each manager or supervisor will be assigned an element of our quality manual. There are 23 elements. We will need 23 individuals or some of us will have to double up and take more than one element. Obviously we will give elements to individuals who normally work in the area that the elements address and have the expertise to address the details. They in turn can pick a team. The team should follow the ten disciplines needed to write a good procedure that we all heard about in our training sessions. I will write up a form with the ten disciplines for teach team to follow. Dennis's operating team along with each of the element champions can vote on the critiqued elements when they are done. I suggest a consensus vote should be required to get elements approved for the manual."

"Sounds like a good plan, Vito," said Dennis. "Why not draft it up so everyone knows the approach? One concern I have, however, is DG—he may have the toughest job, since he will not only have to address our current technology, but the new technology."

"I am not sure," said DG. "Based on the company's timing plan to go for this quality award, all of these procedures and test method write-ups will have to be done con current with the implementation of our new technology. So, unless I misread the timing plan, I think all I have to do is concentrate on the new technology along with the controls, test procedures, an operating guideline, for that new technology. We should be into production with the processes when the quality award is submitted. And since my team has to do this anyway, I may not have to do any incremental work."

"That is excellent," said Dennis. We will need to go through this exercise anyway for the new technology so the disciplines we learned about in training can be utilized and that will even make us look more capable to our customer."

"I see no problem with that strategy," said Vito. "But not everyone in the skunk works or the plant had the same training that we had on building a quality system. So I will take a little survey and get everyone into training that hasn't taken it up to now."

"And I will add that to the budge overrun," said Mary.

With that, Dennis set up a series of meetings that would discuss progress toward the goal of getting a good quality manual and system together so they could meet the audit criteria, not only for the ISO 9000 series of requirements, but also the Baldridge requirements.

Key Take Away Thoughts

Designs of experiments, benchmarking studies, and other tests can be performed to identify a set of metrics. However, when all the data is collected and the analysis complete, sometimes it is better to use the wisdom of the human mind to finally decide on the overall quality metric for your product. A lot of information is not knowledge. In many cases, manufacturing locations have so much information, they find the bigger issue is to recognize the information chain that leads to the data base they need to run the business.

Understanding that wisdom is quality will give you the keys to quality:

- Do what you say you do
- Your perception of quality must be the customer's perception of quality
- You must have a disciplined quality culture—drive the change
- There are four levels of a good quality system—make sure they are consistent with one other
- Use a disciplined approach to developing the quality system
- Understand that a qualified individual must have experience, education, and formal training
- Six sigma levels of quality for all your metrics are the benchmark; less is unacceptable, and zero defects are unreal

Experience Principle #14: Leadership and Learning Is Painful

There must be leadership—and leadership requires experience. However, in today's environment, there is not enough of that commodity called time to develope an individuals leadership abilities. And, without time to gain experience, learning must accelerate. You will have to be fast on your feet—which means you will make mistakes. You learn through mistakes. However, making mistakes in the day to day operation of a plant becomes painful. It can be concluded, and experience will verify this conclusion, that leadership and the process of learning must be painful to be effective. *No pain, no gain.* There is no substitute for experience; therefore, you must get it as fast as you can. In manufacturing that means on the fly. Employees need to plod their way through the ropes and challenges in manufacturing to develop a deep understanding of the dynamics that occur in operating teams, business, and the changing competitive strategies.

Management Must Lead

Manufacturing must take on the leadership role since the buck stops at the manufacturing level and there is no one left. Leadership requires teamwork, shared vision, and most of all, risk. You must disrupt the comfort level of others to be a true leader. If you do not create an environment in your plant where leadership can excel, then your business will slowly die. True leaders create discomfort which must be accepted if your leadership role is to progress.

Leadership means risk. And risk inherently translates into making your boss or upper management nervous. This rarely comes out in books written on manufacturing or mechanisms to pursue productivity. There is, of course, one reason for that: leaders create chaos and discomfort that affect career paths. One writer on this subject named Nietzche stated, "you must have chaos within you to give birth to a rising star." Leaders must break paradigms. They must be mindset busters. I have read many times that changing corporate or plant cultures takes five to ten years. I never wanted to believe this but my experience has shown this to be very true. Continuous improvement in an operation requires changing cultures and the leaders must be hanging out there a long time before the results are recognized. That is why management and supervisors at all levels must recognize this and a plant culture must exist to allow leaders to grow at all levels. When you are at the bottom of the corporate system, one of the bucks that fall to manufacturing is leadership. If there is no leadership in manufacturing, there will eventually be no company or plant.

Some companies destroy a person's career if they are associated with a mistake. This makes leadership painful and stressful. Successful plants protect and encourage people who make mistakes and learn by their mistakes. Companies and plants that destroy a person's career for being associated with making a bad decision will create a culture of anti-empowerment. They will empower themselves to do nothing and shut down their creative skills. However, if a decision made is wrong and the operating team let it be known that they appreciate the risk that was taken, it will have a positive effect on future performance.

Your Mission Is to Create a Leadership Environment

A leadership environment can be developed by empowering people to be leaders. This is not just left as an exercise for management—it must be done at all levels. The lowest level employee, for example the janitor, will perceive the next higher employee such as the machine operator is top management—since the machine operator is the one who controls the quality of their work life. The operator and union think the supervisor or manager is top management—and the mangers think the directors and vice presidents are the top people. It is human nature to attempt to send the leadership buck on every miscellaneous issue up the ladder. People tend to perceive a company has one and only one leader. However, it is far better to have thousands of leaders than one. It is really up to everyone to practice leadership. Plants must create a mindset where their people accept leadership for items they can address at the plant level. That means operating teams must have objectives that create and sustain a leadership environment at all levels.

There are many books written on leadership. One article in the magazine Fast Company summarized 12 characteristics of leadership. I will note them below and add comments as they relate to manufacturing based on this experience principle.

1. "Leaders are both confident and modest. You need a healthy ego to lead, but you also need to be strong enough to check it at the door. Being a leader is not about making yourself more powerful, it's about making the people around you more powerful." Getting ahead in most organizations takes a big ego and management tends to perceive those with big egos as the doers. It doesn't follow, from a career path development, one should help others to be more powerful. The result? Leaders must absorb a lot of pain—it affects career paths.

2. "Leaders are authentic. You earn the trust and respect of the people you work with when you know who you are—you walk the talk." Upper mobile managers on the fast track tend to change their opinions and direction depending on what meeting they are in and who is in that meeting. They walk the talk that plays well with the powers to be. So, it takes pain to stick to your convictions.

3. "Leaders are listeners. It's hard to be a great listener if you're not curious about other people". In American industry, the top person in the room usually does all the talking. In Japan, the top person in the room rarely utters a word. They let the individuals who are most knowledgeable about the subject, their underlings, do the talking. It is very difficult for people in the Western World to keep quiet and listen. It is painful to keep quiet especially if you are the most experienced person in the room. But it must be practiced.

4. "Leaders are good at giving encouragement and they are never satisfied. Leaders are always raising the stakes of the game for themselves and their people." Think about it. If you raise the stakes of the game in a plant, then you also have to perform. You stress yourself. And who wants to create stress for themselves?

5. "Leaders make unexpected connections. They organize and lead conversations among people who don't normally interact with each other. They see the kinds of patterns that allow for small innovations and breakthrough ideas." This is absolutely critical in an industrial environment. You must use the brain power of everyone to get ideas out for productivity improvements.

Many times, you have to force it and listen to a lot of tripe in order to get to some real meaty ideas.

6.   "Leaders provide direction. No single leader is smart enough to know everything. But smart leaders do know how to pose revealing questions." Direction requires a decision and making decisions takes risk. Management magazines have done studies that say two out of three decisions that industrial managers make are wrong. So the probability of making a wrong decision is greater than making a right one. That is why upwardly mobile career path oriented individuals shy away from making decisions. The leader, however, has to take the painful approach of being perceived as wrong. But look to the bright side. Once the decision is identified as wrong, then it can be adjusted and probability improves of making the right decisions.

7.   "Leaders protect their people from danger and expose them to reality. Most people want leaders to insulate them from change rather than mobilize them to face it. That is why leadership is so dangerous." No comment necessary.

8.   "Leaders make change and stand for values that don't change. One job of the leader is to help people identify what habits and assumptions must be changed for the company to prosper." This becomes part of the learning process. And learning like leadership is painful. You learn by your mistakes and mistakes cost money in industry.

9.   "Leaders lead by example. Small gestures can send big messages. Leaders have a fundamental obligation to live their lives according to the principles they espouse." You can't tell a child that smoking is bad for your health if you smoke. Likewise, you can't tell others to be leaders if you're not ready to take the leadership pain pill. If management promotes leadership but then makes leader the scapegoat if failure occurs, they soon will not have any leaders.

10. "Leaders don't blame, they learn. Bill Gates once decided that the Internet wouldn't have a big impact on Microsoft's business—Try, fail, learn, try again." Hopefully, this concept is catching on. In the 50's and 60's, management styles were just the opposite. The most senior individual in the room would question the other meeting participants and sooner or later one would have to say that they did not have the answer. At that point, the individual

would be humiliated by a senior executive. It was perceived that managers were running the show and controlled everything. It doesn't work today.

11. "Leaders look for and network with other leaders. Look for allies, network with link-minded colleagues." It is lonely at the top only if you want to be on a pedestal and if you don't, you have share in the benefits of your actions. You can't take all the credit and that is painful for the ultra ego people.

12. "The job of a leader is to make more leaders. Your ultimate task is not just to be a leader, it is to make more leaders." This means teamwork at the leadership level. When it becomes time to take credit, however, you will have to share the glory with the team. This can be tough.

Successful leadership can be measured when the work force internalizes changes that are being pursued. One quickly finds out that training does not equal internalization. It requires more:

Immersion + Experience + Accountability = Internalization

Most companies train, train, and train but do not immerse the employees in changes to the plant and do not hold them accountable. All of this is needed before an employee internalizes changes to their plant. Once they do, the change is accepted and it can move forward. "Industrialution" is change in a plant and, as noted throughout this book, it just keeps coming which makes leadership and learning so necessary and painful. You can't have leadership without learning. And neither will occur without pain.

People Are Your Most Important Resource

The human brain is the most sophisticated computer ever developed and if you can get all those computers that exist in the minds of your employees connected and working in sequence toward a common goal, there is nothing that can not be accomplished. That is your objective.

Educating, training, and motivating people is the way you connect the minds of the employees. It is difficult, but should be the number one priority for every manager. It is difficult because you need to learn by doing. And doing means making mistakes on the job while running production. People will only learn through the discipline of doing and making mistakes as they go forward. Eventually they must get qualified to do their jobs. Qualified is defined as the following:

Qualifications = Experience + Education + Formal Training

You would never think of scrapping a machine when it fails to produce a good or is running slow. You would have an aggressive "PM" (preventative maintenance) program to not only keep the equipment running, but up to date with the latest modifications. Likewise, human resources require "PM". However, it is surprising how few organizations realize how important it is to maintain the people that work in their operation. Maintaining employees in a manufacturing environment and keeping them at peak performance requires an understand and acceptance of the following:

- People are your most important resource
- People are a manufacturing operation's only long term sustainable competitive advantage
- Productivity happens when people focus on results, not effort
- The future is only limited by an individual's creativity
- Brains/wits are a person's precious resource
- Success vs. failure hinges on the ability to attract the best people
- Success breeds arrogance—do not get into that mode
- Recognize excellence when it happens, not later
- Live the mode of the three Musketeers—one for all, and all for one
- Don't turn people into obedient robots; keep them creative
- The most important thing you can say to people is—thank you
- Doers will make mistakes—address it and get on with the next action plan

You can control how people behave while they are working in your operation, but you can't control how people think. Managers must get each individual to believe and behave as if they were empowered acting only within the constraints of the team. Managers should lead. Each employee should manage and operate like they are managing their job even though they may not have direct reports. This applies to individuals who are not only on a salary payroll, but hourly employees, contract employees, etc. If everyone acts and behaves like the business was theirs, and the future of their family and quality of life depended on it, you will be successful no what you manufacture. Each employee should act like a manager. The more time individuals spend understanding the functions of their peers, working with other employees and overlaying their job responsibilities with others, the more productive the team will become.

You Must Hire Intelligent Resources

Bill Gates, who founded Microsoft, was asked what he thought was the most important thing he learned when growing his company. He said, "hiring smart people is the single most important thing we have done as a company". Does this apply to a manufacturing company—the need to have intelligent hourly and salary educated employees? The answer is yes for both. Expectations for employees are becoming higher with each phase of "Industrialution." For example, understanding of statistics for the shop floor employee is a necessity today. Hiring people who can't add or subtract let alone understand the basic concepts of statistics, will put your operation at a major competitive disadvantage. Theories on flow through manufacturing, constraints in the system, team thinking, etc. are all things that must be understood.

To get the best salary employees, most Fortune 500 companies are looking only to the top 100 Colleges and Universities. The day is coming where you either have or are working on a master's degree or your career will hit the glass ceiling. For the shop floor hourly employees coming into the work place, a minimum of two years of education after high school is becoming necessary. Why? Because the average employee must be somewhat technically trainable in things like statistical process control, computer processing, etc. Employees in their 50's in most companies will tell you they are constantly being trained and the trend has been going on for years. So, a new employee will have to come in with some skills just to be close to the knowledge level of people that have been in the work place for years. When Toyoda opened their new assembly plant in Georgetown, Kentucky, over 70% of the hourly non-professional employees had full four year college degrees.

Several years ago, I stopped at a fast food restaurant with several coupons my children received for drinks and hamburgers. I placed our order and gave the young lady at the cash register (which is really a computer) the coupons to pay for our food. She pushed the button on the register marked coupon for each coupon we gave her. When completed, the cash register screen totaled minus 5 cents. She was at a loss as to what a negative 5 meant. I told her she owed us a nickel. She, in turn, replied that I did not understand. I was supposed to give her money. She said, "I can't give you change when you did not give me any money to begin with." At that point, the manager and three other employees came over to help. Between the four of them, they could not figure out what the minus 5 cents meant on the cash register. Finally, after much discussion and confusion over what was going on, I declared the discussion useless and left. As I drove off, I we could see them through the window still puzzling over the cash register. They could not understand that the coupons were in fact money and instead of coming up with a change amount, the cash register was programmed to put in a negative number when the coupon amount exceeded the amount of the order. Negative numbers was a concept beyond anyone's understanding in that fast food restaurant. What would these individuals do if hired by one of your manufacturing plants and told they had to do statistics and then take the information and analyze it to identify any potential problems? The answer? They couldn't survive and your plant could not afford to employe someone with that intelligence level.

As would happen, the week after the incident at the fast food restaurant, I was in Japan benchmarking and stopped in Tokyo to do a little shopping. I was looking for a little electronic pocket game and found it in a back alley store. I asked the store clerk (in clear English as I did not know Japanese) how much the little game cost. The young lady replied, in clear English, that it was 1500 Yen. Without ever asking, she immediately estimated the cost in dollars in her head without the use of paper/pencil or a calculator. Then I picked up another version of the pocket game, which was 2000 Yen. Again without asking, she said in English, that it was 25% more and then told me the approximate dollar amount. After buying the second game, I told here I thought she was very intelligent being able to juggle statistics and numbers in her head so efficiently. I asked if she was attending college. Her comments surprised me. She said, "no, I am not good enough to go to college." Think about it—this young woman was speaking in a foreign language doing statistical calculations in her head in a money system that was foreign to her upbringing. She had the abilities and mindset for an outstanding employee.

So, who would you want working in your plant on a team that was trying to understand process improvement, through put, cycle time reduction opportunities, etc.? Certainly not the individual who was still lost over the concept that a coupon was money and a negative five meant change due. The young lady I met and her classmates in Japan are filling the manufacturing plants in that country and they are the competition. Examples like this constantly reinforce my experience base such that I believe to compete, you either prioritize who you hire or your plant will slowly but surely lose its future. And that can be painful for those who did not spend the time in school to understand math and the sciences.

How Do You Get People Who Will Become Leaders

Plants and companies who do the best job of obtaining the people with the most potential and create an atmosphere to motive and maintain them will be the most successful. Studies since the 40's in all industries have been fairly consistent when it comes to understanding what drives people. You always want to say money, but money is never at the top and never has been. What always surfaces as two of the top three motivational drives for employees is "being in on what is happening/what the plans are/what is the strategy" and second "having your accomplishments recognized", better known as atta-boys, pats on the back, words of praise, etc. So if you want to build a plant operation with a commitment to the future your human resources and your management group should spend a healthy amount of time in these three areas:

- Hiring better educated, motivated employees

- Keeping employees appraised of the future through state of the plant or business meetings

- Recognition methods, both formal and informal, such as pats on the back

For many years, industry leaders thought that Japan Incorporated had some advantage that motivated the Japanese people to work together in teams. Then, an awful thing happened. Many of these Japanese companies came the Untied States and Europe and started to develop a work force that operated the same way—only this time with American and European employees. They got the same commitment and work ethic that they got in Japan. Once again, lack of leadership in American and European industry raised the ugly truth—management lacked the leadership and people skills needed for productivity improvements to sustain a manufacturing operation and give it a competitive future.

Teams

Jack Welch, the charismatic CEO of General Electric, has said, "we tear all the walls down and put teams from all functions in one room to bring new products to life. One room, one coffee pot, one team, one shared mission. That is how GE developed advanced ultrasound products and the GE90 jet engine." Work groups or what is referred to as employee involvement teams, are the current industrial wave. Why? Because you have to not only change the culture of your operation, but also the mindset of your people. You have to get them to participate in the running of the plant and get their ideas. It takes management to give up some of their authority and control. It makes managers uncomfortable understanding what their role is in such an environment.

Robert Sherwood noted in his writings on teams that, "although there is clearly no path for establishing a high performance, high commitment work team system, the conception, design implementation and day-to-day management of this kind of work system requires consistent and continuous attention." In other words, the process goes on forever. It has to be nurtured and prodded continuously to survive. All issues must be addressed to the team's satisfaction or the team will stop functioning. I found there is one way to tell if a team is being successful and that is to watch the dynamics of the team when they are in session. If all members are contributing and better yet, disagreeing with each other, you know you have a successful team, assuming of course, that at the end of the day, they do get to a consensus opinion.

However, as Robert Lutz states in his book Guts on re-building Chrysler, sometimes a manager has to get up and take command and control over the situation and make a decision. Clearly, this becomes an exercise in ones interpersonal skills. Teams left to wonder off aimlessly will never achieve the purpose of the team which is to get consensus on an issue and make a decision. Most of the pundits on this subject want to kill command and control, which is the old style of management, but as Lutz has stated, "sometimes you need to stop the dialogue and get in there and dictate the decision."

The Learning Organization

All of this leads to what is today referred to as a learning organization. You must start to understand the elements of a learning organization as that is what you untimely want you and your people to aspire to achieve. If you accept the premise of continuous change and new waves in Industrialution, then you have to learn that whatever is accepted today will change. However, the one thing that will not become outdated is the need to have an organization that is in a constant learning cycle.

The five disciplines of learning adapted from <u>The Fifth Discipline</u> by Peter Senge are noted below and must be understood and become part of all the plant's operating teams and work groups are:

Personal Mastery—the practice of continually clarifying one's personal vision for the plant and building capacity to attain it

Shared Vision—the practice of unearthing shared "pictures of the future" that foster genuine commitment, rather than mere compliance

Mental Models—the ability to surface our assumptions, and to make them open to the influence of others

Team Learning—the capacity to think and learn together, which is gained by mastering the practice of dialogue and discussion

System Thinking—the discipline that integrates the others; the ability to see beyond simplistic cause and effect relationships to an awareness of underlying patterns of interrelationships

These five disciplines of learning must be understood by everyone in your manufacturing operation if your are to continuously improve. Once again, Jack Welch, CEO of General Electric, stated "I am convinced that if the rate of change inside and organization is less than the rate of change outside, the end is in sight." That is why the ability of an organization to learn is so critical to its future.

If a plant is to survive, it will have to change its ways of thinking more in the next 25 years than it has done in the last 25,000 years according to Peter Senge. Operational management owns the relationship with people. Open honest dialogue is critical. You must take time to develop trust and relationships, learn from success and failure, respect each other and develop a method whereby constructive recommendations can be communicated and taken in a positive way.

When people leave school, they tend to think they are done with the learning process. But, in fact, working in today's industrial world, learning is just getting started. As noted in the beginning of this book, the industrial revolution has become continuous at an ever increasing rate which means learning must be continuous. This, of course, is why attention (human preventative maintenance) to your human resources is so very important and takes priority in management's time for improving operational effectiveness. John F. Kennedy stated that "leadership and learning are indispensable to each other." Plant operating teams have to address it and it has to be painful.

Learning Disabilities

There are learning disabilities against which a well orchestrated learning organization must guard. These are the paradigms that emerge in the culture of a plant that you are trying to offset.

1. <u>I am my position</u>. Over time people in an organization believe that they are their position and have not concept how their actions or day to day activities affect the outcome of the whole. This leads to a myopic view of the plant as a whole. Individuals who start to work just for themselves and do not cross over to transfer their knowledge to other disciplines and look at the plant as a whole will eventually break down the organization.

2. <u>The enemy is out there</u>. When something goes wrong, something outside the system usually caused it to happen. This belief will stop any solution.

3. <u>The illusion of taking charge</u>. In many manufacturing plants, proactive people are encouraged to tackling problems quickly, but this proactive approach means you have to fight all those enemies of change.

4. <u>Fixation on events</u>. We are conditioned to see life as a series of events and do not view the megatrends. This fixation of events tends to blind people from the trends that are starting to develop when several of these events are viewed and looked at from an interrelated standpoint. This is something a learning organization must constantly fight against.

5. <u>The parable of the broiled frog</u>. We are very good at reacting to sudden threat and crises. But we are poor at recognizing gradual threats to our plant's future. This is similar to a frog that will sit in a pot of water as it

heats up and let itself be slowly boiled to death because it fails to perceive any immediate danger.

6. <u>The illusion of learning from experience</u>. We learn from experience—from trial and error and from our mistakes. But most importantly, we do not always experience the results, since most decisions take a long time to mature when the results, become obvious. The most critical of decisions usually have plant wide consequences.

7. <u>The myth of the management team</u>. Many teams operate below the level of the lowest IQ in the team. People never call themselves a team because they never experience conflict, disagreements, etc. It is thought that a team keeps individuals from learning. Once again, nothing could be further from the truth.

These concepts and illusions occur when people view the plant in a linear way, rather than looking at it as a total system and interrelationship of of all the organization. This can prevent a manufacturing operation from creating a plant with a future.

EP's Story Part #14—Taking Leadership

EP manufacturing has decided to add a satellite facility and bring in new technology. That means, over time, everyone in the plant must be trained. They also expect that they will have to hire more employees. The traditional way most companies have operated was to bring new employees in and let them walk around and observe the experienced people. However, EP knows that will not work, since they know, in order to be successful, the individuals must be knowledgeable on all the technical issues and problems that occur on a day to day basis. Therefore, Bill in human resources went in to see Dennis with a plan he developed after the last operating team meeting.

"I see a couple of issues we have to address on training the old employees and hiring the new, but I have a plan," said Bill.

"I have also been thinking about one," said Dennis. "But let me hear yours first. Maybe you have given this more thought than I have."

Bill started in on discussion on his plan. "As I see it, we will have to hire about 80 people. Before these new employees came in, however, we will give them a battery of tests to make sure they had the math skills and are able to analyze story problems which is necessary in a manufacturing environment."

"Where do you plan to get employees like that?" Asked Dennis.

"There is one hiring trend that I have noted which can answer that question," said Bill. "The Fortune 500 companies absorbed over two thirds of college graduates for profession carriers 30 years ago. Today, they absorb less than 20%. Where do the rest go? Obviously they are being forced down the food chain to lesser jobs that non college educated employees filled prior to this generation—driving screws, sorting parts, driving fork lift trucks, working at fast food restaurants, etc. So I don't think we will have a problem. Today you must install some type of screening process to make sure people your hire can think logically and handle the basic mathematics and learning abilities needed in manufacturing. The screening process I suggest is called a college degree for the salary ranks and a minimum of a two year associates degree for the hourly ranks. Competition is driving this change and you must have the ability to use the minds of your employees if you want to be in the game for the long term. I once had an experience where we had three male employees brought up in the local community in a middle class neighborhood who were asked to measure a dimension on three production samples every hour. Then they were to add up the three measurements, divide by three and mark down the average. What started to happen is sometimes the answers were right and sometimes they did not make sense. Several times production had to be stopped causing downtime, only to find there was nothing wrong. It confused me as to what was going on. However, the problem finally surfaced after several months. None of these three men could add three numbers if the total was over ten. They never learned to add and carry. If the dimensions they got added to something less than ten, then the average made sense. If the numbers added to eleven or twelve, they had no idea what to put down. These are the things that EP can not afford to live with and why many companies have hiring tests based on the knowledge the employees need to know to operate the equipment."

"Okay," said Dennis. "I understand. But going back to my original question, where are we going to find these people?"

"From the local community college," Bill responded. "I want individuals with at least an associates degree which is a two year degree. I will also look for individuals who took courses in math and the sciences. With our pay, I am sure we can have the pick of the community college. Most should pass our test. I just want to make sure we have people that can think."

"I like your aggressive attitude," said Dennis. "That shows leadership and will make us successful."

"Thanks for the attaboy," said Bill. "But you better wait until my program is completed. Besides, there is the second part. As soon as we pick our new employees, I need to train them on the current system and put them into the production system replacing the existing workforce. So, instead of having the experienced floor personnel handling

problems, the new employees will be responsible and we will have the experienced individuals follow them around giving them tips on how to handle situations. They will be put on the firing line immediately. In this way, they will be immersed in the day to day issues before transferring to the new facility, where there will not be any experienced individuals to fall back on. Also, each individual will internalize what is expected of them and how it should get handled. Our labor costs will double for a short time, but I believe it will pay off in the long term."

"I will accept that cost," said Dennis. "But what I want to know is what your definition of internalization is. I'm not sure what you mean when you talk about that word. Sounds like something you read in a book."

"Yeah, I did," said Bill. "But it made sense to me and I want to try it. There is a formula for what I am saying. Let me write it down for you so you can think about it.

Immersion + Experience + Accountability = Internalization

The key here," said Bill, "is accountability. If you remember the last time we hired employees, we had them follow the experienced people around for a week. They were never on the firing line and were not held accountable. They really did not get any experience. When we finally put them on the midnight shift by themselves, it was a disaster. It is kind of like riding in a car. You can sit in the passenger seat and watch the driver but that doesn't mean you know how to drive. It still takes getting behind the wheel and learning."

"I understand now," said Dennis. "I like the plan. Go ahead and get started. But there is a second item. We will have to get some of our employees, if not all, up to speed on the new technology."

"What we have to do is build a training program into the skunk works concept DG started for the new technology," said Bill. "By putting a couple of hourly employees into the skunk works, we effectively started a learning organization. Now we have to expand that. What I would do is start to rotate employees through the skunk words. Let the skunk works team train them. While this is happening we can continue with a few more state of the plant meetings so that you can clarify your vision for the plants future. Eventually, between the two efforts and your one on one dialogue with the employees when you are walking the floor, we will evolve to a shared vision for the future. After that, it is all downhill. We will evolve to team leaning and get to where the whole system thinking becomes consistent with the business strategy. Ergo—internalization. And if we constantly empress on all the employees that your efforts are to take a leadership roll for the plant, maybe we can start to develop other leaders in our workforce."

Dennis had to think about all of this. He then responded. "I think maybe you're the leader and trying to convince me that this will all come together like you planned, which seems like a long shot. But then, why not try. We have to make it work. If plan A doesn't work, I'm sure you will come up with plan B.

"Already have it in the works," said Bill. "But I don't think we will need it."

Key Take Away Thoughts

A highly trained, highly motivated work force working in a team environment, thinking and operating with a sense of urgency can make things happen at an unbelievable rate. To summarize, the following objectives should be engrained in the minds of the plant's operating team:

• Prioritize/hire of degreed personnel for the salary/management ranks

• For blue-collar jobs, pursue people with two years of education after high school or from some technical schools for your hourly skilled trade labor ranks

• Promote work groups or teams and use this mechanism to develop natural leaders from these groups

• Pursue learning for your entire plant organization—learning by doing

Bundling up the elements of human resource planning and management style that has been noted in this chapter and having your employees at the starting gate, you must arm yourselves and your employees with the three facts of life in today's world of manufacturing:

• The world doesn't owe your plant a living—you must earn it

• There are two sides to success—handwork and reward

• You must have a passion to be better

With this understanding in place, your work teams operating, and the plant's strategy well indoctrinated, the logical conclusion is that you have reached the day of rest. Well, unfortunately, that is wrong. You have just started.

Experience Principle #15:
Numbers Lie

This chapter is finance for the non-financial types. You need to understand the elements of a time adjusted return but not necessarily how to calculate it. You need to understand return of sales and assets and that cash flow is everything. Understanding in the world of manufacturing, however, means plant personnel need to go below the numbers and understand what the numbers represent. On the surface, numbers will not tell you what is going on in the system and where the issues lie. You must get below the numbers to find the root causes of cost problems and where the opportunities lay.

How Numbers Lie

The theory that "numbers lie" will not be found in financial management courses. By saying that numbers lie, I mean you need to get below the numbers to see what they represent, which could be just what is expected or could be something totally different. Let me discuss a few examples. Suppose your plant is old, most of the equipment is written off and partially underutilized, and the plant has an opportunity to quote new business. To prepare a cost quote, the plant must develop the fully accounted cost for the product so that you can establish the price and the profit margin. Many companies will use financial procedures that include, in the cost structure, a depreciation schedule of assets employed based on the cost of brand new facilities, even though the plant's equipment has been written off. The thought process is that a good business decision rests on its ability to absorb costs of new equipment if it were required.

The second thing that can normally be expected is that the financial analysts will add burden rates historically assigned to the plant's current products. If you think about it, that is all the analysts have available. These rates include costs for things such as security guards, powerhouse employees, the plant manager's office, controller's office, etc. Here, again the thought process is the same. The decision should be based on the product's ability to absorb all the traditional costs. The results will be a fully accounted cost for a new product based on these assumptions. When the bottom line number is reviewed, you may not be competitive or able to meet what your marketing people believe should be the target price to get the business.

However, let's look at this closer. The assumption is that this plant had some underutilized equipment. However, the fixed costs for this existing equipment is already being absorbed by current production. Secondly, burden rates for items such as those noted above are already being accounted for in the current production. In reality, the true incremental costs for this new business would only be for the added materials, direct labor and some utility costs to run the equipment that is currently on standby. This underutilized facility could take (generally speaking) only a small incremental difference in the number of people to run it whether it is 100% utilized or 50% utilized. As a result, when you take the market price and subtract the cost, you may not be able to quote the business using the historic cost structure. However, it could be very profitable if you assumed only the incremental costs to develop the quote.

Did the numbers lie? Those of us from the school of non-finance management would say yes; those from the schools of financial management may say no, assuming better opportunities will come. My experience, however, has shown that business opportunities rarely come along using historic cost data if your plant operates in a very competitive environment. I have seen financial decision matrixes that doubled the fully accounted cost of new business when in reality it didn't occur. But you only know that if you can get below the numbers. Most financial decisions tend to be made based on a plants current cost structure and not future projections of costs. This, of course, occurs as the financial decisions do not acknowledge the industry is changing and how the cost structure may be or can be changed. In my example, if the plant was half empty, the fixed cost assigned to each product would be double what it would be if the plant was full and the equipment fully utilized. This may be the reason the plant can't get new business. However, if the plant looked at getting new business using an incremental look, eventually it would be full. Then, if the fixed costs and burden structure was re-allocated across all the products, the operation could be profitable.

A second example, which may clarify this a little better, is a non-manufacturing example. This is a true story that hits the key points of this discussion. The individual in this story, whom I will call Joe, was in the real estate business and owned small apartment buildings. He had an opportunity to buy a building far bigger than the ones he had owned. Since he was getting a little out of his league, Joe decided he better understand the detailed costs to run the building before he made his decision. The building was going to be sold at auction to the highest bidder. However, as is normal, the auction required a minimum starting bid. When Joe reviewed the books, as did all the investment groups planning to bid on the property, it was obvious that the costs were extremely high over the years and rents would not generate enough cash flow to offset the costs. It appeared on the surface that there was not going to be any profit. The logical conclusion was purchase of this building would be a bad financial decision except. Joe looked deeper into the numbers.

The apartment was owned by the U.S. Government's Housing and Urban Development department; known as HUD. In the previous two years, HUD authorized and completed replacement of the elevator system for the building plus carpeting, stoves, and refrigerators in each apartment. In total, they replaced everything of any cost that a new owner would have to concern himself with for the next 10 years. Second, he found the manager of the building either did not competitively bid for services and construction projects, or he was getting a kickback from the contractors. It didn't matter what the reason was, Joe knew the going construction costs and was able to estimate the cash flow he could expect if he ran the building his way. The third and most important item was that everyone in the apartment building received their rent as part of a government program. The rents were subsidized. That meant the government would send all the rent checks directly to Joe and he would not have to pay someone to collect them or evict bad tenants, losing the rent money in the interim. And last, after talking to some of his competitors, he realized that they only looked at the available financial sheets and did not get below the numbers. So, it was a good bet they would walk away and not bid on the property, which meant he could risk going in at the base bid price.

What looked like a money pit with nothing but problems was in fact a cash cow with little or no management issues in the foreseeable future—the numbers lied. In the end, Joe was the only one who bid on the property. Joe was the only one that bothered to get below the numbers and find out what they meant. As a result, Joe got the building at the minimum bid price. To end the story, he got his money back in 18 months with no added outlay after purchasing the building as he predicted. Now, he has a good eight to ten years of collecting the profits. One more note. The government guaranteed the loan so there was no problem getting a loan.

This example was not manufacturing related, but should give you a clear understanding as to what I mean when I say that numbers lie. In an industrial environment, however, it gets a little more complex and is less obvious.

Profit Versus Cost Centers

There are profit centers and there are cost centers. Some companies want their plants to be cost centers and let the marketing and sales organization drive the profit picture. Even if this is the case, those of you who are inside the walls of manufacturing must understand the cost elements of your business as well as the pricing elements.

Companies who want their plants to be cost centers do not realize that working in a cost center environment is like working in a communist state—one needs the motivation of profit to drive costs down. Without it, you are just like indentured servants and you do not necessarily make the right decisions. For instance; assume one of the products you were manufacturing was a constant source of downtime, quality issues, etc, and it constantly drove down your financial performance. An aggressive plant management team would allocate as much burden against that product as possible to make it look like a looser to profit center folks, thereby hoping they outsourced the product line. Cost centers are drivers to make performance to budgets. Keeping business in the plant is not a driver for a plant operating team. They will always want to get rid of a borderline product to make their plant look better.

Likewise for a new product, there is no motivation to keep the investment down or take a risk with aggressive cycle times, quality objectives, etc. If you are a cost center, you are going to ask for more of everything—investment, the best equipment, budget relief, etc. You will build top of the line tools that require little to no maintenance to make your life easier for you in the plant by reducing day to day downtime issues. My experience has shown that this is natural if you're a cost center—it must be human nature.

You want your plant to be driven by a profit motive even if there is some company organization above the plant level that accounts for the final profit picture. Items such as economics and increases in material costs are things a cost center does not address. A profit center, however, will drive those cost increases attempting to keep them to a minimum. Because, once again, only at the manufacturing level is there enough understanding of the details of the business to allow creative alternatives to increased costs. For this reason if no other, keeping all levels of manufacturing in a mindset that profit is everything is the most effective way to keep costs down and create a driver for productivity. Communist countries ran their state owned companies as cost centers, while democracies motivated their people and companies to run as profit centers. Communist countries, as we have seen, suffered the consequences. It might seem strange comparing plants to political systems, but it is not. Plants are no different. In manufacturing, you must get to root causes to solve problems. Profit is the motivator.

Activity Based Costing (ABC)

Profit will become automatic after price is established, since your fully accounted costs are, at a point in time, what they are. But understanding the details of the cost structure are key to making decisions for future business. And the only way to do that in an industrial environment is to dig into activity based costing. It may not be the accounting system in your company, but it is critical for making plant decisions. If your required to use other accounting systems, then you will need to overlay activity based costing. In manufacturing, you use numbers to make decisions. ABC forces you to do the homework necessary to understand what lays below all the numbers—then the numbers won't lie.

ABC is equivalent to zero based costing, which means you look at each element of your manufacturing costs to put together your income statement. Now if you run just a one product manufacturing operation, then you have activity based costsg in place since you know each element of cost applies to that product. Where it gets complex is when you make several products. The finance community has historically binned costs for a manufacturing complex for ease of manipulation of the numbers. Prior to computers, ABC was complex and would have most likely required a small army of accountants. Today, once you identify your cost elements and set up your ABC system, then the ability to control the system becomes easy and it is the only way in today's environment that a manufacturer can afford to operate. Competition is rough in any industry and unless you know the details of your costs, you can not win. Traditional systems allocate the same overhead to high volume and low volume product lines which is never the case. The ABC view looks at every cost element and bins it according to value or contribution to that product. Dr. Robert Kaplan of Harvard University contrasted the views on how costs behave as shown in Figure 10.

The reason this is so important is that you want to understand where you are making money and where you are loosing money. Sometimes the answers are totally opposite of what you would think. ABC gives you those answers or at least gets you a better view of your cost structure and where you should spend your time and money. ABC is just another way of saying you have to grind out the details and go through all the work needed to understand the business.

Traditional View	ABC View	Examples
Variable	Unit	Direct Labor Direct Material Machine Hours
	Batch	No. of Setups Move Materials Inspections
Fixed	Product	Maintenance Engineering a Process
	Facility	Depreciation/Capitilization Utilities/Overhead
	Administration	Plant Manager Plant Staff Allocations

Figure 10

It also changes the way you view things in a plant in a way that gets you into the cost structure so all the elements can be understood and addressed. As in Figure 11, you know you are spending money on salaries but what you really need to know is what the salaries for those people are buying.

The key of costing in a plant using the above approach is to take all the department expenses and break them down into activities. Traditional financial management wants to understand the costs but necessarily the activity that is being performed. Telling a plant team that X dollars is associated with a department's equipment depreciation does not give them any indication of cost savings opportunities. But tell them the bulk of the depreciation is on a specific facility that happens to be underutilized, you now have an understanding of some real opportunities.

The Income Statement

Given you have done a good job of identifying all the activities, you also need to develop an income statement to accompany the activity based costs. Now we don't mean the stereotypical income statement that you find in stock reports such as Figure 12.

Example: A Typical Material Control Department

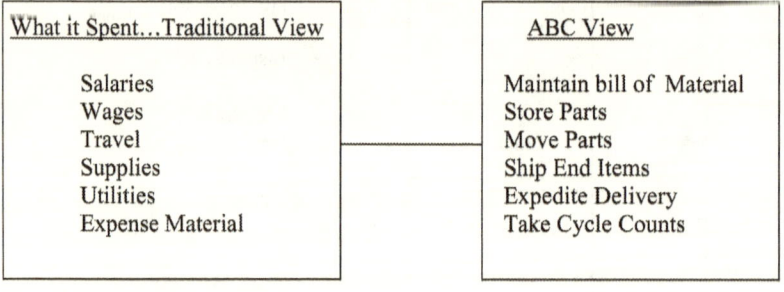

What it Spent...Traditional View	ABC View
Salaries	Maintain bill of Material
Wages	Store Parts
Travel	Move Parts
Supplies	Ship End Items
Utilities	Expedite Delivery
Expense Material	Take Cycle Counts

Figure 11

Generic Income Statement

Revenue
Cost of Goods Sold
Economic Profit
Selling, General Administration Expenses
Operating Income
Interest Expense
Net Income before Taxes
Taxes on Income
Net Earnings/Profit

Figure 12

You need a down to earth detailed income statement that addresses location and sources of your costs. These become the meaty items you need to understand and are also the items that you want to use when benchmarking yourself against a competitor.

Detailed Income Statement

Sales by Region A
Sales by Region B
Intra-Division Sales if Appropriate
Inter-Company Sales if Appropriate
Total Sales

Raw material
Purchased Parts
Purchased Parts from Other Company Locations
Freight In-bound
Freight Outbound
Premium Freight Costs—Anything Out of the Ordinary
Import Duty
Export Duty
Direct Hourly Labor
Indirect Hourly Labor

Variable Salary
Non-Variable Salary
Overtime
Off-Day Shift Operating Premiums
Warranty
Scrap Costs
Rework Costs
Other
Total Variable Costs

Allocations
Indirect Hourly Specific to the Product
Indirect Hourly Non-Specific Like Security Guards
Fringe Benefits
Salary Specific
Salary Allocated
Other Overhead
Depreciation
Leases
Project Expense
New Product Launching Expenses
Design Costs for New Products
Tools amortized over the life of the product
Tools Expensed Out
Marketing Costs
Sales Costs if Different Than Marketing
Administration
Other Such as Union Costs
Total Fixed Costs

Inventory Adjustment

One Time Currency

Interest of Money

Humane Resource—i. e. Medical/Disability/Workers Comp.

Royalties

Joint Ventures

Total Other Costs

Profit Before Taxes

Figure 13

If you don't have your costs broken down to the level noted in Figure 13, your task becomes cumbersome. But it must be done. Once your understand you cost structure, you can establish a base for the total cost of running the plant.

For instance, you may be making year over year profit improvements because of savings the suppliers are passing on or they may not be increasing their prices but have the opportunity to increase your prices. This is good news and appears you have had productivity improvements when in reality you have done nothing. The risk is that the opposite could happen. Your suppliers could increase prices and you have no ability to pass it on to your customers. Then, profits would deteriorate. This is one reason why you need to be looking at all elements of a plant's cost structure and working in each area to reduce the individual item costs buried in the income statement.

I have found that in most manufacturing operations, the operating teams need to have a clear picture of how they are going to achieve productivity improvements in the following fiasco year months before the end of your current fiasco year. They need to identify at least 50% more actions than required if they expect to meet tasks. Not all opportunities will materialize. Experience has shown that if you do not have at least more cost reductions in the system than your target, you will not meet your tasks. That can only be done if you get below the numbers and understand what each one means and where there are opportunities.

Playing the Budget Game

Budget preparation should come after and only after you understand your cost structure and have established productivity targets that you need to meet in order to keep your business viable. Targets are those elusive objectives that always appear impossible to meet at the beginning of the financial counting period. They should always be stretch targets. Ones which no one knows how to meet. This keeps the operating team on their toes and usually requires some thinking out of the box. By thinking out of the box, I mean clearing your head of the paradigms that have evolved over time and looking for new ways of running or processing the manufacturing operation.

What is a good target? It depends on the industry you are in and if you have matured or are still growing as an industry. If an industry is mature and there is a lot of competition, than 3-5% year over year improvements are a difficult task. If you are in a growing industry, the sky is the limit. Usually targets are not necessary, as you mindset is to keep up with the growth curve and hold market share.

Budget targets/tasks are established as a report card—you need to know how you are doing in each category. The bins aren't important in themselves, but without binning the budget into various categories, you will not know which elements are out of control and which are being maintained. If budgets do not have tasks, then you will be guaranteed that there will be no improvement. If there is to much task, the same will occur. When people have an impossible task and can't win, they will not try. The trick is to establish a manufacturing budget with tasks that can be achieved or over achieved with some effort—people need to know they can **win** if they try. Therefore, budget setting becomes an art in itself. There are no ground rules. Experience and historical performance in your industry is the only key.

One good example of tasking a process was given to me by an old time industrial engineer. His budget task for the upcoming year was to take labor cost out of a conveyor assembly line by refining the process time studies. His approach was to spend the first week talking to the people who worked on the line. He had coffee with them at their breaks and got impute as to the constraints on the line and where they thought it could be improved. In this way he got the confidence of the people plus their ideas. This gave him most of his ideas on how to improve the line. During the second week, he took his stop watch and time studied the operators to verify that their perceived bottlenecks were accurate. When he got done, he sat down and reprocessed the line breaking some of the bottlenecks and increasing the line's output. But what he did next is key. He established a line rate that would allow the people to meet the day's production output 15 minutes before the end of the work day. He knew that they could beat the new rate even before he established it on the line. However, he didn't establish an optimum rate. Why? Because he knew, after 30 years of being a industrial engineer, that if the people had a rate in which they could win and beat the clock, allowing them to sluff off for 15 minutes, they would hustle just to get that small unofficial break. Good parts out the door was his measure and the result desired by all manufacturers. What line balance did this industrial engineer's experience show would end up with the greatest number of pieces out the door—a line rate which could only be achieved in 8 hours or one which could be achieved in 7 hrs and 45 minutes? The answer was the 7hr and 45 minute line rate. The people could win and on a day to day base, would work harder if they knew there was chance of winning. This industrial engineer knew that in the real world a rate on paper which should give you a maximum output in 8 hours, in reality will give you less parts out the door than a rate of 7 hours and 45 minutes. On paper the numbers lied. Reality was the opposite.

Cash Flow is Everything

This should be engrained in every employee's head. With an established budget and targets established, the other financial element that comes into play in manufacturing is called project spending. To stay ahead of the game you have to constantly spend money and those require returns if they are to be understood. Some businesses are sensitive to the amount of money invested and some are sensitive the cost savings or price improvement that can be achieved with spending the funds.

When you get your paycheck you pay your bills, budget living expenses, and allocate so much for savings and entertainment. If you don't, unless you have a rich uncle, you know the results. So everyone in some form or the other understands cash flow. However, when that same individual walks into a manufacturing operation, somehow he/she seems to forget this basic law of survival as it is usually someone else's money. Most people believe the company or plant they work for "is and always will be" and therefore the treasury function is something that either doesn't exist or there is some god that allows them not have to worry about cash flow.

This can happen even at the top of a Fortune 500 company. Lee Iacocca was President of Ford Motor Company before he left to run Chrysler. When he got to Chrysler, the company was on the verge of collapse and Iacocca had to approach the government for a bailout. Chrysler's cash flow was non-existent. Years later Iacocca made a statement in a speech I attended that cash flow was just a number on a piece of paper when he was at Ford. He never once thought about the treasury function. At Chrysler, that all changed the first day he reported to work. Had every plant and every operating team in Chrysler had the understanding and urgency to manage cash flow with the ramifications indelibly branded in their brain, it is unlikely the company would have ever gotten to the depths they did before the bailout. That is why everyone, no matter what level they are in a manufacturing company, should understand the cash flow situation and how they can help. Once they do, it will be surprising how people will respond when you say you can't afford to invest in this facility, new technology or have to meet budget targets in order to keep the business sustainable. Manufacturing operations must always emphasizes cash flow.

EP's Story Part #15—Cash Flow Concerns

Dennis called Mary and DG to his office to discuss the cash flow problem that he perceived when they would get into production on the new technology. He said, "I am worried that when we complete the building addition, get this new equipment, and hire the added people, we will end up with a negative cash flow, which will raise a lot of bells with our parent company. I also want to know how we are going to price this new technology."

Mary responded. "Let's take one problem at a time. Cash flow. The company will accept two years of negative cash flow since we are adding all these new assets. But after that, they will start to get nervous. So, when we do our pricing, and DG does his process layout, it all has to come together so that we start going positive on cash flow by the third year. Now, as I said, the key to that is in the cost and pricing detail. So we have some homework to do."

"My plan," said DG, "is to start up the new technology using the new equipment in the building expansion. Assuming this takes off, we will migrate the technology into the older equipment in our current building using our current resources. By the third year, I am assuming we will have the plant totally converted. Then we can spread out

the costs over the entire operation. It is a challenge, but I think we can do it. Will that help the cash flow issue, Mary?"

"Directionally you're dead on," said Mary. "But I have to do the financial analysis. What we need to do is get a team of my people along with some of your process engineers and do a downtown job of activity based costing. In other words, we will have cost every element of this new technology. That way by the time it is across the plant we will know for sure what our true accounted costs will be. That then leads us to pricing."

"Can't we back into pricing?" asked DG. "Why not figure our costs, add our profit and that is the price?"

"It would be nice," said Dennis. "But that is not the way the world works. Our customer's product, the toys they make, are priced based on competitive information and what the market will bare. They in turn, take out profit and establish a target cost. That target cost is broken down into its elements and we will end up with a target price. Now since we already have a good feel for that price, I think we can assume pricing for this new technology. If the returns aren't there, well—DG has to try harder."

"I should be worried about that comment," said DG, "but I'm not. I believe that our fully accounted cost will be less with this new technology since we will be saving some processing steps. If we can get the same price we get for our products today, our profit should go up and that will help pay off the new equipment."

"I agree with DG," said Mary. "I have done some guess-ta-mits and I think we will be okay but we need to understand all the cost elements before I can say we can pull this off. Also, why not get a price increase?"

"I already thought about that," said Dennis. "As you know even though Barb is our logistics manager and not a marketing person, she is off doing a little marketing for us like we discussed early on when we first discussed our game plan. In her little pitch, Barb is telling the staff marketing folks that this technology is so new that they can advertise it. Based on the skunk works estimate, we can guarantee a longer life for the toys. That has to be worth something. Early indications are that Barb has marketing agreeing and they are getting excited. I think we will get a price increase."

"All right, cash flow and returns are starting to look better," said Mary. "I better keep track of Barb's efforts."

"Well," said Dennis, "it looks like EP manufacturing is going have a plant with a future. We have a game plan and a strategy and it looks like it will pay off. A lot of work has already gone on, but it will never stop. It looks like everyone should be congratulated. I think we are going to have one big party after we start production with this new technology."

"Oops," said Mary. "Another budge hit not expected."
Everyone laughed.

Key Take Away Thoughts

You need to run your operation as a profit center, even if your parent corporation requires you to be a cost center. It doesn't. You can report out as a cost center but run the internal operation and decision making functions as a profit center. This will motivate the resources and people tend to want to run their piece of the business like anyone else. And that is why you also need to emphasize that cash flow is everything. Make it simple for people—tell them they have to pay the bills. How do you do that without cash?

Most of all, the key thing to remember in manufacturing is to be successful you have to get below the numbers. You must understand every element of the income statement and what makes up each of those elements. You can't just accept the numbers. You must know how they are generated, what goes into the numbers and what they mean. If you do, you have a chance of getting your pulse on the operation. That is the only way you can control its destiny.

Conclusion...Industrialution Experience Principles

The Experience Principals are comprised of 15 theories that my experience has shown function independently of the continuous changes in the industrial environment. They are principles that will get you through the ongoing reinvention that has become the norm in industry today.

It is critical for the reader to understand that each of the principles are interrelated and must be played out in total if your plant is to be successful. The principles are like instruments in an orchestra. Each has its own purpose and taken by itself, does not make a recognizable sound. Together, however, they form a symphony orchestra where you are the conductor. How you execute the principles is critical and must be thought through. Examples are given in the chapters on each of the 15 principles.

A synopsis of each principle is summarized below. This synopsis should only be read after going through the detail in the previous chapters. It should be kept handy and re-read periodically to keep your mind focused. The game never ends; it just keeps going and you are forced to play to survive.

EP 1...Define the Game

The objective of the game is to win. Winning means staying in business. Staying in business means keeping up with "Industrialution" and being passionate about it. The game players all work in your company and have equity in the outcome. As you experience each principle in this book, you will build on the game plan. You must examine these annually if you are to manage your manufacturing facility wisely. This, of course, is difficult to accomplish, You must do this during your day job—which is to get a product out the door. However, remember the following:

- Identify your plant's expertise—is it based on product, process or material?

- Understand you have to play the game of corporate politics to survive

- He who makes the rules, rules

- Assume nothing

- Play the game passionately

Hopefully, you will understand why you must, as a manufacturing type, never take your eye off the business part of running a manufacturing plant.

EP 2…Bureaucracy Brinkmanship is Critical

Staying ahead of the bureaucracy takes leadership. You must increase your flexibility. Eliminate words like should and shouldn't, right and wrong, and do not use phases like I agree or do not agree. You want to change your focus to meet objectives and solve problems by closing your eyes to the day to day clutter that takes your mind off the long-term objectives.

- Remember you are part of the bureaucracy

- Plants are empowered more than they think when it comes to doing business planning

- Develop a business plan for your plant; Re-do it every year

- Play the games necessary to keep your plant in the best light

- Think/plan for two years ahead

- Get involved in how costs are binned

- Don't let the bureaucracy decide on your future

You also need to remember that while you are working on the future of the plant, you need to accomplish short-term objectives. A manufacturing team needs small wins in order to keep motivated to continue. Get resistance to change out in the open so you can deal with it and address the root cause of people wanting to stop you from making changes that will keep the plant ahead of the bureaucracy. Many times your underlings will link with the old ways of doing business since it is safer and they hope it won't affect career paths.

EP 3...Benchmark or Self-Destruct

Benchmarking doesn't always give you the answers and may just confuse you more. The reason benchmarking becomes so important for the manufacturing person is the discipline one must follow. It will make you realize that you never truly understood your own system. And if you don't understand your own system, you will not be able to follow the first two experience principals. It is also important to remember that benchmarking must be dynamic—it never stops. You're always looking at data at a point in time and not where your competitor is going. He may doing the same thing you are—trying to figure out where you are going. And it could be to a technology place where you already were. It is a natural tendency to think someone else knows more than you know.

- Benchmark your own process first

- Benchmark other industries that may have similar processes

- More data can be obtained from a company that is not a direct competitor

- Pick your team from all disciplines, no two from the same discipline

- What you don't find is just as important as what you do find; note it

- Benchmark a plant that is not perceived as state of the art; you may be closer to them than you think

- Benchmark several facilities on the same trip because, it gives you perspective

- Read the walls. All real data in a plant can be found on walls, and machines

- Always end the day with a re-cap meeting. Note all visual observations

- Develop an action plan to follow-up on your major observations

The soft information, knowledge that does not have a direct metric, can be the biggest find from a benchmarking trip.

EP 4...Identify the Customers Itch and Scratch It

Marketing types have developed systems and processes to identify customers and their needs. A manufacturers roll is not all that organized. Sometimes there is only one customer and one itch but it can destroy your reputation.

- Identify your customers

- Find out what "itches" them—what problems are they are sensitive about

- Identify the root cause. Fix or contain the root cause—this will scratch the "itch"

- Develop a disciplined approach to problem solving

- Communicate the disciplined problem solving approach to the customer

- Communicate the solution

- Make sure the sub players, customers not necessarily in the loop, are kept informed

- Follow long term performance to verify the solution to the "itch" is permanent

If there is a potential "itch" which could surface, you need to get at it as soon as possible with some preventative approach. This is called predictive planning.

EP 5...Be Technology's Fastest Follower.

If you are not a leader or a fast follower, you're not in the game. And if you're not in the game, you will not have a plant or product with a future. Technology is moving at a constant pace. Continuous improvement is the requirement of the day. If you can't address this experience principal, then you haven't done your benchmarking homework. Equipment suppliers aren't technology leaders in processing and they are not the ones to whom you should talk. You need to take what they have and adapt it for your needs and than keep those little nuisances of change in your hip pocket.

- You must stay at the forefront of technology for your operation

- You have choices, the best approach is to be the fastest follower in technology

- To follow, you have to understand technology when you see it

- If you don't have it, it is new technology as far as you are concerned

- Try to maintain your equipment and keep up with technology—the best of all worlds

- Two years ahead of the competition is as good as it gets

- Make sure your plant has and continues to maintain a technology roadmap

- If you are so far behind that you can't run fast enough to be a fast follower or you facilities constrain your abilities, then you must develop a leap frog technology which is one that is way beyond what the industry is doing—obviously this takes risk

You must benchmark technology to understand your plant as well as the competition. Experience will tell you that you can either drive your plants future or you will be relegated to live with the outside forces which constantly attack your status quo and like Armageddon, you will always be wondering when it is going to get you. In the end remember what Peter Drucker said: "in a competitive global area, costly mediocrity goes out of business. Don't solve problems, pursue opportunity." In other words, you better be technology's fastest follower or you're going out of business.

EP 6...*Communicate, Communicate, Communicate.*

Assuming you have defined your business and launched your new product, plant, technology, or added resources, you are ready for the day to day manufacturing agenda. What is it? What do good operating teams do to assure performance to their objectives and customer "wants". There are several things:

- Understand that employees want in on what is going on

- Don't manage; lead

- Be a change agent

- Manage communication just like any other project

- Understand Accountability—make sure everyone knows they are accountable

- Understand the cycle of change. Build it into your program management system

In day to day operations, things happen so fast that you must meet daily or weekly and talk through all the issues. The discussion between all attendees is critical to get everyone's input. These can be short, but must be mandatory attendance. Political correctness is not what you want in a plant meeting. If your daily meetings include individuals who constrain communication, then the meetings have the wrong attendees. If you are the problem, listen. If your boss is the issue, you should let him know that the meetings will be more open and productive if he or she is not in attendance. People are more open when in a meeting with their peers. If managers or supervisors are in the meetings that rate performance of other individuals who are in the meeting, then the discussion becomes somewhat guarded. In a manufacturing meeting, arguing, disagreements, yelling, pounding on the table, and general venting are very important. You can't do that if supervisors or managers of the peer ground attend. <u>Harmonious (Zen like) daily plant meetings are a sign that either your team is not open to discussing the issues, or you have a very loose budget</u>—another one of those little experiences which is rarely, if ever, wrong or very far off base.

Communicate, communicate, communicate. It can not be highlighted to often. Understand communication takes time and put it into your planning.

EP 7... Worship the "4Ps".

Product, Process, People, and Plant are the 4Ps. Never change all four at the same time or disaster awaits. If you remember nothing else, remember this one principal. If at all possible, all you want to do is change one "P" at a time. However, as "Industrialution" is accelerating, you may have to risk changing more than one of the "Ps" and that requires leadership. It all depends on the game you must play to stay ahead. Changing two "Ps" is manageable, three is a major risk, and four is a guarantee of a disaster.

- Never change all "4Ps"

- Keep a plant small—small means manageable

- Understand the key decision items that can change your decision matrix as to what country in which to build a plant—unions, environmental, transportation, tax structure, material availability, tax structure and credits

- If you don't sell product in a specific country or do not plan to, don't build in that country. And the corollary; if you want to sell in a country you will most likely have to have some form of manufacturing there

EP 8... The Buck Stops at the Bottom—Manufacturing.

When all the planing, strategizing, marketing issues, E-Mail, and designing are complete (in other words when the paperwork shuffle stops), you must physically produce parts and add value in order to pay the salaries of all the marketers, planners, money changers, talkers, etc. When the buck stops, it is the manufacturer who must have the discipline to overcome the slippage in timing. Manufacturing must get resolution on design disagreements, make gut decisions on facilities required for the volume and mix assumption, get the hardware in place and get product out the door in time with no quality issues The buck truly stops at the bottom which is manufacturing in today's world. You need to make sure that you handle the "buck" when it comes flying your way.

- Beware of sales projections—you may want to protect your facilities by adding your own confidence factor into the projections before you commit resources and investment

- When time is up, and you have to get going and make plant changes, you may have to grab the design and run even if it is not completed and hope you can adjust later

- Don't let the buck rattle around in your plant. Grab it and make someone accountable to address whatever the issue is that comes with buck

- Stop and plan. Plants tend to lean toward the quick fix, since they are always under pressure

- Be creative. Use the authority levels you have to address issues and get the ball rolling

- Insurance for the plant is a good thing, insurance being the expenditures for "if come" programs and technologies that will offset investment in the future.

However, there is always the risk you will end up spending the money needlessly

EP 9…Champion Best Practices

What are best practices. They are those many routine methods of operating that must be done in a plant in the best way you know how. These are items that must become ingrained in the minds of the employees and become part of day to day routines, items such as housekeeping, safety, ergonomics, operating patterns, the application of computers and microprocessors on the plant floor, and supplier relationships. Championing a set of best practices is like teaching your child to bush his/her teeth. You want it taught as gospel until it becomes a routine or at least takes very little time to monitor. You want best practices to occur automatically. However, like any other practice, if it is not checked periodically and a metric established that reports on progress, they will die out or become paperwork exercises with no real teeth. That is why you must champion them.

- Housekeeping tours force discipline. Clean plants are more productive

- Safety pays besides being the right thing to do for yourself and your employees

- Ergonomics has long term ramifications; people will hurt themselves if you let them

- Be aware of operating patterns on productivity. Address it with your workforce

- Beware of the computer. Always assume you do not need another software package or computer and make sure it gets justified from a value add standpoint. The trend to add computers for the sake of computers can bury you with so much information you find the data necessary to run the operation

EP 10…Stress Drives Lean Manufacturing.

Lean manufacturing has become the latest buzz word when discussing inventory reduction. Lean has different meanings to whomever you talk to. Generally, however it means inventory reduction. What isn't talked about when pundits of inventory reduction discuss lean manufacturing is the "how to" achieve that position. In my experience, it takes stressing the system. You stress the system by making decisions early on such as buying limited facilities and shipping containers—the minimum amount. This forces the team to operate the plant assets at significant up times. Another approach is to allocate limited floor space for in-process and end item inventory. Forcing inventory reductions beyond the mind-set of the plant populace will force the operating people to address issues of downtime, lost production, quality, etc. Inventory masks problems. The historic concept of reducing inventory to reduce the financial affects of carrying costs are really minor compare to what can be saved when you look at the inefficiencies that exist in a plant and how they surface when inventory is lowered. Tasking inventory reductions must be driven down until it becomes painful. If it isn't, you haven't reduced the levels far enough.

EP 11…Flexible Workers Add Flexible Capacity

You can study the needs for automation versus human intervention and put a financial tag on each approach. In the end, however, it is your gut feeling from your previous experiences that will tell you the answer. But here again, it is an area where the plant teams are the only ones who know the answers.

- Keep a process simple

- Always ask yourself if it is wise to automate

- Remember, your best defense against the seven losses (breakdowns, set-up time losses, start-up time losses, tooling losses, speed losses, minor stoppages, and quality issues) is a flexible workforce

- Volume and mix changes are guaranteed. Make sure you can be fast on your feet with a workforce that can handle the changes

Just remember three words—flexibility, flexibility, flexibility.

EP 12…Time Is the Key to the Game

Time is the key to the game in today's world of "Industrialution". It is not easy to understand the underpinnings of time. The 'how to' is what is difficult to comprehend and implement. Remember:

- Time is money

- Measure time using MTT (Manufacturing Cycle Time) and PTT (Plant cycle Time)

- Robustness is time

- Purchase reliable equipment—reliability is time

- Workgroups are critical—they reduce the time to identify problems

- Equipment efficiency must be understood

- Monitor the seven losses

These are keys to time management. Your time elements are the underpinnings that will make you successful. An expert in the game of billiards will take a shot based on setting up a subsequent shot. He will never shot without addressing the following move. The same strategy is necessary to be successful at playing chess. A chess player has several moves formulated ahead of time and may even have the entire game formulated—but remains agile and can adapt if his or her opponent makes an unexpected move. Time is the biggest enemy at staying the course and maintaining a plant with a viable future. So you must have moves planned well ahead of time.

EP 13... Wisdom Is Quality

When all the data is collected and the analysis complete, it is necessary to use the wisdom of the human mind to finally decide on the overall quality metric for your product. Since those who read this book represent different industries each will have far different metrics to address. In many cases, however, most manufacturing locations have so much information they find the biggest issue is to recognize the information chain that leads to the knowledge they need to run the business. Remember the keys to wisdom and you will have the keys to quality:

- Do what you say you do

- Your perception of quality must be the customer's perception

- You must have a disciplined quality culture—drive the change

- There are four levels of a good quality system—make sure they are consistent with one another

- Use a disciplined approach to developing the quality system

- Qualified individuals need experience, education, and formal training

- Six sigma levels of quality for all your metrics are the benchmark Less is unacceptable, and zero defects are unreal

EP 14...Leadership and Learning is Painful

Management must lead. The buck stops at the bottom—manufacturing. Therefore the only way up is for the plant operating team to take the lead, disrupt the comfort level of others and create an environment where the business can grow and thrive. However, true leaders are out running to a different set of objectives and breaking paradigms—which generally makes a boss uncomfortable.

Education systems tend to spoon feed knowledge to people and parents tend to want their offspring not held accountable for the learning process. Unfortunately, the manufacturing plants get these people and to make them useful employees, must have training programs as part of the budget. However, in industry where the buck stops and you have to build a product, it also stops with people not being held accountable. People have to perform and have to be held accountable and responsible. To get a product out, plant people must learn. And the only true way to learn is by making mistakes. If you do not make mistakes, you don't learn. In a plant, mistakes are costly and result in daily performance issues. So, it becomes painful especially since most employees know you can't afford to keep making the same mistakes. So, you better learn. If your team doesn't make mistakes and can handle the day to day routine without issue, you're not stretched far enough. You need to stress the culture further. A highly trained, highly motivated work force working in a team environment, thinking and operating with a sense of urgency can make things happen at an unbelievable rate. Every member of the team must be immersed in the mission of the plant and trained until it hurts.

- Prioritize/hire of Master degreed persons for the salary/management ranks

- For blue collar jobs, pursue people with two years education after high school or from some technical schools for your hourly skilled trade labor ranks

- Promote work groups or teams and use this mechanism to develop natural leaders from these groups

- Pursue learning for your entire plant organization…learning by doing

EP 15…Numbers Lie.

This principal will not be found in any finance manual. However, if you dig deep into income and loss statements, you will find a lot of binning has taken place that is not necessarily relevant to the way a manufacturing operation is run. Decisions become the wrong decisions if you use general financial assumptions. You need to understand the detail of what it costs to make a product and using "Activity Based Costing" is about the only way you can dig into those details. The answer to financial performance is in the details and unless you understand and have a feel for the numbers, they will lie to you and mislead everyone as to the future of the business. Non-finance operating people should understand one metric if nothing else and that is cash flow. The details of the financial management of the plant can be left to the controller but each and every person should understand and be aware that cash flow is a metric to be followed. If you always have positive cash flow, your plant and company will always be in business. This does not mean you can not absorb a year or two of negative cash flow, but when this occurs everyone in the manufacturing area should understand it and the reasons for it. If it is not for things such as major investments, then you have a problem. Also, it can only be negative for a short period of time.

Synopsis

These are the "Industrialution's Fifteen Experience Principals." Microprocessors are driving knowledge and this accelerating knowledge is changing the way we must run our manufacturing plants. Time has become the lost resource which industrialist had at their disposal during the first industrial revolution. It is the resource that allows one to gain experience. With time to learn from experience shrinking due to "Industrialution", new manufacturing techniques and global business requirements are driving managers of industrial operations around the world to adjust their techniques without the ability to gain knowledge from their previous decisions. They will not be able to learn by their mistakes and grow with the business. As a result, the major growing problems of industrial globalization will be manager's inability to spend enough time to develop experienced human resources to run new manufacturing sites.

Most manufacturing operations are good at addressing one or two things at a time but to be successful, you must manage all the elements. The experience principles are a method, if practiced religiously, that will contribute to achieving what every plant operating team must strive for—**a plant with a future and one that has productive throughput in a time frame that exceeds the expectations of its customers.**

0-595-31204-7

www.ingramcontent.com/pod-product-compliance
Lightning Source LLC
Chambersburg PA
CBHW030921180526
45163CB00002B/428